In the Potter's Workshop

In the Potter's Workshop

EXPERIENCING THE DIVINE PRESENCE IN EVERYDAY LIFE

Robert P. Vande Kappelle

WIPF & STOCK · Eugene, Oregon

IN THE POTTER'S WORKSHOP
Experiencing the Divine Presence in Everyday Life

Copyright © 2019 Robert P. Vande Kappelle. All rights reserved. Except for brief quotations in critical publications or reviews, no part of this book may be reproduced in any manner without prior written permission from the publisher. Write: Permissions, Wipf and Stock Publishers, 199 W. 8th Ave., Suite 3, Eugene, OR 97401.

Wipf & Stock
An Imprint of Wipf and Stock Publishers
199 W. 8th Ave., Suite 3
Eugene, OR 97401

www.wipfandstock.com

PAPERBACK ISBN: 978-1-5326-8124-0
HARDCOVER ISBN: 978-1-5326-8125-7
EBOOK ISBN: 978-1-5326-8126-4

Unless otherwise noted, Bible quotations are from the *New Revised Standard Version of the Bible*, copyright © 1989 by the Division of Christian Education of the National Council of the Churches of Christ in the United States of America. Used by permission.

Manufactured in the U.S.A.

> We are the clay, and you are our potter;
> we are all the work of your hand.
>
> —Isaiah 64:8

> I went down to the potter's house
> and there he was working at his wheel.
> The vessel he was making of clay
> was spoiled in the potter's hand,
> and he reworked it into another vessel,
> as it seemed good to him....
> Just like the clay in the potter's hand,
> so you are in my hand...
>
> —Jeremiah 18:3, 4, 6

Contents

Chapter 1: Introduction | 1

Chapter 2: Why I Am Not an Atheist | 7

Chapter 3: What Does it Mean to Experience God? | 22

Chapter 4: Varieties of Religious Experience | 37

Chapter 5: Experiencing God in Everyday Life | 48

Chapter 6: Experiencing God through Jesus Christ | 61

Chapter 7: Experiencing God through Prayer, Meditation, and Silence | 77

Chapter 8: Experiencing God through Worship, Community, and Scripture | 95

Chapter 9: Experiencing God through Pain, Suffering, and Loss | 106

Chapter 10: Experiencing God through Nature | 121

Epilogue: The Kingdom of Heaven | 129

Bibliography | 141

Index | 145

CHAPTER 1

Introduction

God, like nature, abhors all vacuums, and rushes to fill them.

—Richard Rohr

UNLESS ONE IS AN atheist or an avowed skeptic, the highest human aspiration is to experience God in this life, to encounter the divine in some objective and direct way. For such encounters would affirm our uniqueness as human beings, confirm our relatedness to our Ground of Being, and sustain our sense that we live in a purposeful universe.

In 1972, in the wake of the turbulent sixties, a decade in America filled with hope but also with social and political chaos, two books appeared with intriguing titles. The first, by the well-known evangelical author James I. Packer, was titled *Knowing God*, and the second, by the renowned charismatic theologian Morton Kelsey, titled *Encounter with God*. The publishers heralded these works as landmarks in the field of spirituality: *Knowing God* as potentially the most significant book of the year, and *Encounter with God* as one of the major books of the era, viewed as providing the kind of effect in the field of theology that Copernicus had achieved in the field of astronomy.

Both books, however, fell short of the hype, for neither delivered on the promise of direct experience of the divine. *Knowing God* provided biblical knowledge *about* God, reinforcing the traditional evangelical emphasis on the life of godliness as exemplified by trust and obedience, faith and worship, prayer and praise, submission and service. According to Packer, God is known when one lives in the light of scripture: "this, and nothing else," he writes, "is true religion."[1] Packer's book, more about religion than about God, is primarily an exposition of traditional evangelical Christianity rather than a primer on intimacy with God. For those who wished to know God directly and experientially, the book was a disappointment.

1. Packer, *Knowing God*, 16.

Where Packer's book missed the mark, Kelsey's *Encounter with God* delivered, if one is interested in phenomena such as speaking in tongues, prophetic utterances, healings, visions and dreams, and related charismatic activity, for which it provides intellectual rationale. Such signs and wonders, rejected by many traditional Christians as overly emotional, subjective, and contrived, were widely experienced in biblical times and in the early centuries of Christianity. They can be found in other world religions, however, and need not be viewed as uniquely Christian. Furthermore, mainstream Christians continue to debate the value of this activity, particularly since it was unknown or ignored by most Christians throughout church history. This leaves us with more questions than answers, questions such as "Can God be known directly, uniquely, and authentically apart from charismatic activity?" and "In what manner can non-charismatic Christians experience God?"

A third approach, widely practiced through church history, seems more promising, namely, encountering God through prayer and meditation. In this regard, helpful works are *Intimacy with God* and *Open Mind, Open Heart*, practical books on "centering prayer" written by Thomas Keating, a Roman Catholic monk in the Benedictine tradition. While Father Keating charts a course that promises intimacy with God, he focuses on devotional disciplines that leave many practitioners short of the goal, more a means than an end.

After some frustration and disappointment, we return to our question: "Can God be known directly and personally by humans?" Apart from a handful of mystics, who throughout history have claimed oneness with the divine, the question seems misguided, for the Christian tradition, by enlarge, directs us to a lesser yet equally valuable goal, namely, to experience the presence of God rather than the person of God. Such a goal—indirect rather than direct intimacy with the divine—is not only commendable but actually attainable by the majority of Christians, and it is this goal that we address in our study. In this regard, we will be led by a seventeenth-century monk named Brother Lawrence, an unlearned Carmelite brother who authored a series of Conversations and Letters published as *The Practice of the Presence of God*. This brief Christian classic contains the reflections of an individual who sought to make the love of God the end of all his thoughts and actions, no matter how trivial. Seeking God in all things, he desired God alone and nothing else, not even God's gifts or blessings. For Brother Lawrence there is no higher goal, nothing equally commendable. Can this be our goal as well?

INTRODUCTION

The closing words of Richard Rohr's influential book, *Falling Upward*, are perhaps his most important: "God, like nature, abhors all vacuums, and rushes to fill them." Viewed from a spiritual perspective, the goal of life is to live directly in the presence of God, experiencing God's magnificent love and will in all things, an emptying process described by the framers of the Westminster Shorter Catechism as the "chief end of man," namely, "to glorify God and enjoy God forever." If our task on earth is to glorify God, the benefit of such a way of life is the consequent enjoyment of God, an attitude and way of life available to believers here and now and not simply in the afterlife.

In his book, a persuasive discussion of the spiritual stages of life (which he calls the first and second halves of life), Rohr addresses his readers directly: "Nothing can inhibit your 'second journey' except your own lack of courage, patience, and imagination. Your second journey is yours to walk or to avoid." Pain and self-emptying, he adds, are part of the deal, but only "for the sake of a Great Outpouring."[2]

This talk of the first and second half of life is not new. It has been embodied for centuries in the scriptures, tales, and experiences of men and women who found themselves on the further journey. In this second half of life, people have less interest in judging or punishing others, or in harboring superiority complexes. By now these things have shown themselves to be useless, ego-based, and counterproductive. Daily life now requires discernment more than kneejerk response toward either the conservative or liberal end of the spectrum. In the second half of life one focuses less on commandments and precepts and more on changing one's own attitude, on forgiving others rather than criticizing or finding fault.

Life is more spacious now, the boundaries of one's life having been enlarged by the addition of new experiences and relationships. This may be what Ken Wilber meant when he said that "the classic spiritual journey always begins elitist and ends egalitarian." In the second half of life one is less concerned with mastery of independent dance steps and more with just being part of the general dance. Such people have no need to stand out, make defining moves, or be better than others. Life is more participatory than assertive, and there is less need for self-assertion and self-definition. In the second half of life people live in the presence of God. In that reality, the brightness comes from within, a reflection of the divine that is more than adequate.

2. Rohr, *Falling Upward*, 160.

Those who live in the presence of God no longer have to prove that their ethnicity is superior, their group the best, their religion the only one that God approves, or that their place in society deserves special treatment. They become less preoccupied with amassing goods and services and focus on giving back to others a portion of what they have received. Their concern is no longer to have what they love, but rather to love what they have. When one meets such a shining person, one knows that he or she is surely the goal of humanity and the delight of God.

What Rohr calls the second journey or the second half of life I call "practicing the presence of God." Such a way of life involves a coalescing of one's will, attitudes, and priorities around one goal: "To glorify God and enjoy God forever." What this means and how it is accomplished are the subject of this book.

Spiritual and Psychological Approaches

In this scientific age, Christians need to resist the tendency to reduce spirituality to psychological terms. While there are similarities of interest and areas of overlap between spiritual and psychological realms, they represent fundamentally different disciplines. Psychological methods and attitudes are far more objective and tangible than their spiritual counterparts. To formulate too strict a separation, however, to divorce mind from spirit, is artificial and obstructive. We are human beings, with body, mind, and spirit all reflecting aspects of our unified being or soul. To consider the spirit (the dynamic force of being) without addressing the mind is unhelpful, like caring for the mind while ignoring physical health. Thus, some kind of balanced attitude is required.

The most obvious difference between psychotherapy and spiritual formation is that the former focuses more on mental and emotional dimensions such as thoughts, feelings, and moods, while the latter focuses more precisely on spiritual issues such as prayer, religious experiences, and the sense of relationship to God. While some kind of balanced attitude is needed, we must beware the danger of collapsing mind, emotions, and relationships under the general rubric of spirituality. Likewise, spirituality must avoid focusing attention excessively on extrasensory psychic experiences or on dream analysis. In such cases the means have surpassed the goal.

For people on the spiritual journey, the goal is not spiritual experience in itself. Exciting and dramatic experiences can actually distract us from our goal of constancy toward God. Gerald May makes this distinction in *Care of Mind, Care of Spirit*, his study on the psychiatric dimension of spiritual direction: "Although spiritual journeys often begin in the context of experience, and although experiences constitute major vehicles of insight, growth, support, and service along the way, the goal of the journey can never legitimately be experience itself. The goal is beyond experience, and has to do with our actually becoming who God means us to be and doing what God means us to do. Experiences can sometimes be a helpful means towards this end, and they can sometimes get in the way. But they are never the end in themselves."[3] Our task is not to trust experience but to trust God.

For those pursuing spiritual goals, it is a good rule of thumb to ask questions such as, "What does it mean to focus on God?" or "What things are preventing the working of the Holy Spirit in my life?" All human experiences can be said to be spiritual in the larger sense, but spirituality focuses most clearly on those areas that reveal the presence or leading of God in one's life.

Thus, primary attention should be given to personal prayer life; to practices such as meditation and contemplation and other ways to simplify and slow things down; to awareness of God's presence, absence, or callings; to experiences of fundamental meaning; to personal longing for God; and to the multiplicity of factors that seem to help or hinder fullness of living in God's presence.

In general, psychotherapy encourages effective living, and its values often reflect prevailing values in the surrounding culture. For example, psychotherapeutic approaches focus on helping patients achieve autonomous mastery over self and circumstance, whereas spirituality seeks liberation from attachments and self-surrender to the discerned power and will of God. In stricter forms of psychiatry, the physician assumes the role of healer while the patient remains a compliant object whose deficiencies are corrected. In more humanistic psychotherapies, therapist and client form a healing team together.

In spiritual formation, however, the true healer, nurturer, sustainer, and liberator is God, and the disciple is a hopeful channel of grace. In their spiritual pursuit, seekers must reject two extremes, the temptation to play God (that is, substituting personal mastery for surrender to divine will), and the risk of apathy, whereby seekers avoid their own graced potential for action by refraining from doing anything at all. If examined

---

3. May, *Care of Mind*, 38.

closely, both extremes reflect excessive willfulness, the former by aggrandizing personal power, and the latter by restricting it. The one denies the transcendence of God; the other denies God's immanence and human responsiveness to God.

The question is deceptively simple to ask yet exquisitely difficult to answer, "Am I truly seeking to do God's will, or mine?"

Questions for Discussion and Reflection

1. Select one or more of the following options that best characterize your understanding of what human beings can hope to achieve in their experience of God:
   a. indirect knowledge of God
   b. experience the presence of God
   c. experience occasional encounters with God
   d. contact with God
   e. intimacy with God
   f. union with God
   g. none of the above
2. Do you tend to think of God as "out there" (that is, as different from us and as distant), as "nearby" (as accessible to humans), or as "deep within" (as involved in your life)? Explain your answer.
3. Are you satisfied with your current spiritual state? If not, where would you like to head spiritually, and what adjustments do you need to make to get there?
4. Are you living in the first or second half of life spiritually? Explain your answer.
5. In your estimation, can human beings know God directly and personally? Support your answer.
6. If humans can know or experience God directly, does the goal of experiencing the presence rather than the person of God seem like a copout or like a goal worth pursuing?
7. Have you had an experience or encounter with God or with Jesus Christ? If so, how would you describe it?
8. *For personal reflection*: In your spiritual quest, are you truly seeking God's will, or your own?

CHAPTER 2

Why I Am Not An Atheist

The trouble with most people is that they are not agnostic enough.

—MORTON T. KELSEY

DOES GOD EXIST? Is there a deity somewhere within or beyond the known universe? The only true answer is nobody knows for sure. No ordinary human being, whether in the past or in the present, has been able to offer conclusive evidence either for the existence or the nonexistence of a deity, however defined, envisioned, or experienced. With regard to the existence or nonexistence of God, all of us are agnostic. Some of us lean toward theism, others toward atheism, but beyond one cannot go.

As the Christian scriptures make clear, all God language and God experience is faith based. Whatever one believes or disbelieves, the supportive argumentation is merely an extension of that person's faith orientation, presuppositional base, or intuitive worldview. As we learn from modern philosophy, all so-called proofs for the existence or nonexistence of God are but footnotes to one's assumptive stance. Meaningful human discourse or reflection on the existence or nonexistence of God requires acknowledgement of assumptive premises and starting points.

The next concern when speaking about the existence or nonexistence of God involves identifying the specific understanding or view of God being affirmed or denied. Quite frequently thoughtful theists and atheists find themselves agreeing on caricatures or stereotypes of God they mutually reject, such as God's supposed omnipotence and omnibenevolence, contradictory concepts at best. Unless one upholds extreme or untenable views such as biblical inerrancy or doctrinal infallibility, all God-talk is figurative in nature and all Christian theology provisional. If you find a statement about God helpful or relevant, adopt it with caution and examine it carefully. Conversely, if you find a statement about God problematic or irrelevant, approach it with an open and inquisitive mind before you modify or reject it.

Perhaps your spiritual experience is similar to mine. You have known about God since your childhood, having been taught that God is loving, gracious, just, forgiving, almighty, and omnipresent. You believe in God, and you would even say you love God. At times your love of God may have been passionate and intense, but overall more lukewarm or cold than hot. You consider yourself spiritual, and you have practiced the disciplines of devotion such as attending church, reading scripture, meditation, and giving of your time and money to church and to those in need. Your prayer life has been habitual, though mostly limited to mealtime or to situations of anxiety, uncertainty, or perplexity. Although there have been times when you prayed regularly and faithfully, even then God seemed silent and remote.

You long for God, desiring intimacy with this source and ground of your being, yet you feel you do not know God directly. Your religious upbringing taught you a great deal about God, and perhaps you had a conversion experience. There may have been times when you felt God communicating with you or through you—perhaps through a vision, a dream, an insight, or in ways that had no other explanation—yet your desire for intimacy with God went unfulfilled. In the end, however, all of these seem somehow unconvincing, for the impulse, initiative, and motivation appeared more human than divine. You desire something more, and are unsure that all this spiritual activity is but a human contrivance, a way of meeting some human need for meaning and transcendence.

The apostle Paul was commenting on human spirituality in general when he noted that "we see through a glass, darkly" (1 Cor. 13:12, KJV). Yet inadequate vision of the divine need not prevent us from occasional glimpses of light in the darkness. While the human experience often takes us into great deserts of doubt, dryness, and lostness, we need not remain there. How often we see only our failures and forget those times when we have been channels of divine love.

My spiritual journey—described in detail in the opening chapters of *Beyond Belief* (2012) and in the introduction to *Iron Sharpens Iron* (2013)—follows a religious paradigm that views one's faith story as a journey through three stages: precritical understanding (also called primary naiveté), critical understanding (a skeptical stage reflection the collision between one's childhood beliefs and those of modernity), and postcritical understanding (also called secondary naiveté). While many individuals experience all three stages fully and chronologically, as I did, some remain in the precritical phase—a state in which they accept without question those values and beliefs they received from parents and other significant authority figures in their lives. For others, this state is short-lived, abandoned in their adolescent years or during college or early adulthood, a time in life when they began questioning the existence of God and other inherited religious beliefs.

While many seekers today choose to remain in this critical phase, perplexed by the competing views promoted by multicultural traditions, world religions, and by secular worldviews, those who persevere in their faith journey discover that agnosticism and atheism are not final destinations but rather temporary stops. That has been my experience. Though my engagement with the critical perspective began seriously during my graduate and postgraduate studies at Princeton Theological Seminary, I did not fully commit to that phase until the final years of my midlife, well into the second half of my teaching career at Washington & Jefferson College. Then, for a two-week period, I became an atheist. During that brief period I became convinced that God, however conceived, did not exist. Strangely, despite a sense of deep loss, I found the awareness exhilarating, for I had based this conclusion on my own experience. For a year I had immersed myself in scientific and philosophical literature, searching for an understanding of God in these academic disciplines. I took seriously the conclusions of Richard Dawkins and other "new atheists" and found convincing the methodology of former evangelical John W. Loftus outlined in The Outsider Test for Faith. This device encourages people from various faith traditions to assess their truth claims from the perspective of an outsider and with the same level of skepticism they use to evaluate other faith traditions. Applying this methodology to my own religious perspective, I spent a year subjecting my religious beliefs to logical scrutiny, temporarily replacing faith presuppositions with rational and scientifically verifiable premises. This undertaking infected me with rational thinking, labeled "the philosopher's disease" by a Zen Buddhist sage. While the critical phase brings euphoria, closure, and a sense of freedom to some, my experience left me scarred, emotionally and intellectually, a condition exacerbated by my religious upbringing, my vocation, and my ordination vows.

Beyond Belief reflects my thinking during this stage, short-lived in my case. Subsequent writings, including my biblical commentaries and works on theology and spirituality published since 2013, represent postcritical reflections. Whereas critical thinking leads to religious skepticism and withdrawal from religious activity, postcritical believers participate in religious rituals as meaningful but optional. They hear ancient biblical stories as "true" and recite the creeds sincerely while knowing them as not literally true. That distinction is what separates postcritical from precritical understanding. While practitioners in both phases exhibit similarities, speaking and even worshiping alike, the differences are profound, making it virtually impossible for someone who has embraced critical and then postcritical thinking to revert to precritical understanding.

Speaking as a postcritical Christian, I am heartened by the words of Morton Kelsey, a counselor, spiritual director, and therapist who reflected on his own agnostic phase when he wrote: "To help the questioning, the agnostic and the atheist, [spiritual counselors] need to be people who have struggled with doubt themselves and have come out on the other side with a meaningful faith. . . . The trouble with most people is that they are not agnostic enough; they are not consistent in their agnosticism and do not go into it far enough to see its darkness and agony."[1]

In a letter to one he was guiding, Abbé Huvelin, one of the most accomplished spiritual directors of all times, spoke from personal experience when he wrote: "In faith we have just enough light to follow the right way, but on either side there is an abyss." The abyss of agnosticism, manifested in cosmic rootlessness, can cause unbelievable pain and suffering, as we learn from the writings of atheistic existentialists such as Sartre and Camus. Feeling alone in a meaningless world, however, often results in more than existentialist despair. It has emotional and physical consequences as well.

In his autobiography, *Memories, Dreams, Reflections* (1963), and in his earlier works, such as *Modern Man in Search of a Soul* (1933), Swiss psychiatrist Carl Jung tells how he was jolted from the rational, materialistic agnosticism of his medical training. A colleague of Freud, he broke with Freud after discovering there was a nonphysical dimension or reality, observable to anyone who would take the trouble to experience it. It was, he said, as experienceable as were the two moons of Jupiter to those in Galileo's time who were willing to look through his telescope. Jung believed that one of his most important therapeutic tasks was to free people trapped in the constricting materialistic outlook of modernity and open them up to a more adequate view of reality. He viewed the person caught up in materialism as more sick than amoral or immoral.

1. Kelsey, *Companions on the Inner Way*, 61.

One of Jung's important contributions to modern psychology and theology was his recognition that the inability to believe in anything, or the belief in a meaningless world, could be classified as disease or sickness and could cause as much damage as childhood trauma, acute tension, or a dose of poison. Believing that one has no meaningful place in the universe is not only a disease or sickness, but it can result in actual emotional and physical illness. Numerous devastating emotions may result from the sense of living in a hostile or indifferent universe, ranging from fear, anger, and stress to loneliness and depression. Studies show that 60 percent of those under continuous stress actually suffer some serious physical illness within twelve to eighteen months.

Much of the drug dependency of our time is surely related to the psychic sense of meaninglessness in the universe, coupled with the fear that no one loves and accepts us we are. From this perspective, life seems unfair, particularly if it ends with extinction at death. When there is no friendliness in the universe, there is little reason to expect it from other human beings, and less reason to reach out to others. Our separation from social meaning can lead to isolation, loneliness, and depression, which makes us susceptible to contamination by the fear, anger, depression, stress, and hopelessness of others. Psychic infection usually strikes below the conscious level and is difficult to deal with consciously. Rebuilding seems hopeless, and people tend to give up on life, inwardly and outwardly. How can human beings overcome inner anxiety and rage without a sense of purpose and the hope of some meaning in this world and beyond?

One of the functions of the church is to provide a decompression chamber into which we can step out of the negativity and hopelessness so rampant in our society. However, when the church fails to offer an environment of love, meaning, and concern, both human and transhuman, and when it becomes caught up in its own survival, reflecting the fears and suspicions of its weakest members, has it not lost its way? If salt has lost its savor, of what value is it?

The Inadequacy of Disbelief

If we remain within the framework of a meaningless materialistic world, how do we control the effects of destructive emotions such as fear, anger, stress, loneliness, and depression? Without therapy and medication, we simply can't. And even these solutions tend to be temporary, for they don't really target the problem. They merely result in dependency. Without divine assistance, there is simply no way out of the materialistic maze, although it should be noted that right- and left-brain studies show that women are more balanced and less one-sided than men, and often not as defeated in finding meaning as men. However, as we learn from psychiatrists and therapists such as Jung, the cause of much mental and physical sickness is rooted in agnosticism and unbelief. Many of Jung's patients were brilliant scientists who suddenly found that life had lost meaning. This realization left them unable to cope with life and led Jung to the conclusion that among all his patients in the second half of life, that is, over thirty-five, every one of their problems was in some way related to finding a religious outlook on life.

Many years ago William James noted that the inability of people to believe and be converted to religious faith was often intellectual in origin. Afraid to trust their instincts, they became tied to pessimistic and materialistic beliefs, which led them to view faith as something weak and shameful. Intellectually speaking, people should question blind faith and total disbelief, but they should also remain open to valid and helpful alternatives.

Reason, particularly when used as an extension of subjective assumptions or fears, or when based on the views of someone else's authority, can be unreliable and untrustworthy, as modern philosophy teaches. Few people nowadays are convinced of the existence of God by purely rational arguments or "proofs." Skepticism can be a good thing, even of reason, for by relying on reason alone people can prove nearly anything they wish to prove, particularly if their starting point is erroneous. For example, many today accept the assumptions of postmodernism, the Zeitgeist of our day, affirming in conscious and unconscious ways that no final truth exists and that reality is ultimately ambiguous, open-ended, and contradictory. Succumbing to logical reductionism, they disavow objectivity altogether, affirming that what some call truth is nothing but opinion. Thus, they conclude that there is no objective truth, but only "truths," which are essentially subjective preferences and opinions. The loss of absolutes results in relativity and uncertainty.

During medieval times, as evidenced by the contributions of Thomas Aquinas, Christian theology and faith became tied to one or more system or rational thought. This approach, deductive in nature, was formulated by Aristotle, and during the medieval period it became the basis of scholastic theology. Euclidian geometry and basic logic, with its use of syllogisms, illustrate this method, for here one starts with axioms and proceeds to absolute and certain conclusions. But what happens when the axioms are subjective or faulty? Immanuel Kant, the late eighteenth-century German philosopher (1724–1804), saw the logical fallacies in deductive thought and pointed them out with relentless clarity. He understood that logic could not unlock the secrets of either the subjective intellect or the objective physical world. According to Kant, human knowledge results from the interaction of two realities, the phenomenal (physical reality) and the noumenal (non-physical reality). Caught up in a materialistic worldview, Kant believed that only phenomenal experience could be described, and that its understanding could be probed exclusively by reason.

Questioning all authorities and traditions of the past, Kant and his fellow Enlightenment thinkers substituted a virtually unbounded faith in human reason. Kant's "Copernican Revolution," as it has been called, was to reverse the process by which knowledge occurred. Rather than believing that one's mind is influenced by the objects and events it experiences through the senses, Kant maintained that objects and events we know through experience must conform to the operation of the mind. The phenomenal world (the external and natural realms), since it exists apart from our experience of it, is thereby unknowable to the human mind, as is the noumenal world (the spiritual and supernatural realms), meaning that knowledge of God, the soul, and the afterlife are unattainable to human beings. Since the finite mind cannot experience or know infinite things, the best it can do is to postulate or infer their existence. By assuming a sharp dualism between phenomenal and noumenal reality, Kant radically redefined what could be known. Thinkers before him, such as Plato and the church fathers, had assumed that both realms could be known, but Kant limited knowledge only to the phenomenal realm, and even that knowledge to be severely restricted.

Despite Kant's pietistic upbringing, he became known as the father of theological liberalism, a view that denies divine revelation altogether. Kant's dualism between noumenal and phenomenal reality led to modern skepticism, which limits knowledge to what can be apprehended only by means of the senses, and denies that spiritual reality can be known at all. The effect of Kant on liberal Christian theology has been enormous. His philosophical approach plunged generations of seekers after knowledge into an "abyss of subjectivism."[2]

---

2. MacKenzie, "Kant's Copernican Revolution," in Hoffecker and Smith, *Building a Christian World View*, I: 289.

The uncertainty left by Kant stimulated the idealistic philosopher Hegel to develop his own dialectic. Through his method one starts with any thesis (such as Kant's), and allows it to turn to its antithesis. Hegel's antithesis of Kant became the view that all reality was spiritual in nature, meaning that everything manifested absolute mind. Hegel's views became the rage of the middle nineteenth century, a landslide reaction to the agnosticism of Kant and to the even more pervasive agnosticism of the naturalistic and materialistic perspective that swept through Europe at that time. Karl Marx later adopted Hegel's thesis to develop his theory of dialectical materialism, which affirms that only matter exists, a view that became the basis of communist thought. For all idealistic ideologies, intelligence is the supreme value. In Hegel's case, an abstract force guides history, not a divine intelligence.

Hegel's intellectual idealism was in harmony with another method of finding certainty about reality and its ultimate nature, the method of René Descartes (1596–1650), who analyzed the nature of experience through the lens of methodical doubt. Descartes began the history of modernity with his *Cogito ergo sum* ("I think therefore I am"), thereby precipitating what L. L. Whyte described as one of the most colossal blunders of modern thought, making knowledge dependent upon logic and the thinking self. Descartes's efforts resulted in a new starting point for human knowledge, self and logic, rather than God and faith. This shift in priority produced uncertainty about what to believe or not to believe. While Descartes was not a skeptic, his view led to a world in which skepticism flourished. Thus, modernist humans found implausible the idea that there could be supernatural intrusion into human life, and that this could undergird a theology of experience.

Varieties of Disbelief

People reject the meaning that religion provides for many different reasons. One modern option, called *positivism*, is prevalent in our scientifically minded culture. Positivism as an attitude or approach to life assumes that human beings are limited to knowledge of physical phenomena, and that such knowledge is relative and not absolute. Positivists argue that nature has no purpose or essence to shape its direction or development. The assumptions of positivism were formulated by French philosopher Auguste Comte (1798–1857), whose efforts to reshape society along positivist lines resulted in the academic discipline of sociology. Societies that regard humans as merely physical beings tend to treat them accordingly, as figures to be manipulated and controlled.

Related to positivism is *materialism*, a reductionist point of view prevalent in the hard and soft sciences and in much of the existentialist literature of the twentieth century. Existentialism places greater emphasis on what people do than on what they think. Presupposing that there is no God, soul, or spiritual reality, atheistic existentialism declares every person "free" to act as he or she wishes, making of themselves whatever they choose to be. Theistic existentialists such as Kierkegaard, Dostoyevsky, and Berdyaev disagree. Believing God to be the ultimate source of reality in the universe, they argue that people discover their essence not through adherence to themselves but rather through commitment to God.

A third view common among many former churchgoers is *defensive or reactionary agnosticism*. People who exhibit this perspective give up on organized religion or the religious life because of extreme views they encounter from believers who hold literalistic interpretations of scripture and religious dogmas that lead to exclusive understandings of Christianity, particularly those that focus on a vindictive God and on the agonies of hell. Many young adults indicate they have adopted the skepticism of existentialism and positivistic science to escape the guilt and terror espoused by Christian fundamentalism. Their unbelief is quite different from materialistic rationalism. People brow-beaten by well-meaning but poorly informed Christians are not reacting consciously to Christian belief but rather unconsciously to belief of the wrong kind.

There is yet a fourth form of atheism, found commonly among psychology students or those of the psychiatric profession who have been influenced by *behaviorism* or by skepticism found in Freud's pessimistic view of human nature. Though Freud affirmed the existence of the psychic dimension, he believed it was conditioned by an unconscious death wish, an irrational sexual desire, or a repressive superego. For Freud, only human reason possessed any meaning or hope, but even reason was powerless to overcome internal psychological forces. He believed religion represented an immature, regressive return to the comfort and shelter of the womb, a view he presented in his influential work *The Future of an Illusion*.

Another influential modern thinker, Friedrich Nietzsche (1844–1900), glorified the naked will to power by ridiculing the traditional virtues of love and humility found in Christianity. Offering yet another alterative on how to think and live, he described the ideal of hubris (self-pride) as a way to live powerfully and influentially in the modern world. The idea of making one's will supreme, at getting ahead no matter the cost, and of taking from life whatever one can, became the belief system of Nazism and Adolf Hitler's personal philosophy. Unfortunately, most international politics and much national policy is based on this attitude. History shows the futility and disaster caused by this approach.

On the whole, if one's view of the universe (whether held consciously or unconsciously) is that of deterministic materialism, it is almost impossible for that person to take seriously the religious life or worldview of Christianity. Of course, some Christians opt for blind faith, throwing away their rationality entirely, as is done in most fundamentalist sects, but this extreme is not reflective of mature Christianity. It is possible to present the Christian message in a way that does not violate intelligence, and that is our intention. Traditional Christians often find their religious convictions stretched during times of sickness, uncertainty, or personal crisis. Rather than threaten or reduce our faith, such events can actually strengthen faith and expand awareness of the divine (this topic is discussed further in chapter 9).

During the twentieth century, science became increasingly dissatisfied with rational materialism as a comprehensive answer to the nature of things, thereby transforming and challenging many cherished scientific beliefs. Freud and Jung offered new hypotheses about the nature of reality that had much in common with the classical views of Plato and the church fathers. Jung, in particular, opened the eyes of many to an understanding of the world that had been lost to most Westerners for several hundred years.

During the twentieth century, Jerome Frank and Roger Walsh showed the importance of faith and the value of spiritual discipline for the health of the mind, emotions, and body. Likewise, Andrew Greeley gave evidence of the correlation between emotional maturity and mystical experience. In addition, Loren Eiseley and Pierre Teilhard de Chardin demonstrated that natural selection does not account for all the data of biological development. Parapsychology, too, has come of age, providing evidence of nonsensory data. In 1969, after years of rejection, the Parapsychological Association was accepted into the prestigious American Association for the Advancement of Science. This acceptance is an indication that the scientific community has come to believe that human beings are not limited to the five senses. Mystics, as Richard Rohr reminds us, "often intuit and live what scientists later prove to be true."[3]

In his 1962 book, *The Structure of Scientific Revolutions*, T. S. Kuhn, a trained physicist and one of the most influential historians of science, introduced the concept of "paradigm shift," demonstrating that modern science does not provide nearly the certainty that scientists had formerly thought. Likewise, Werner Heisenberg, one of the greatest revolutionaries of modern science, has written that science has discarded many concepts that it thought were final and certain. Using his uncertainty principle, Heisenberg affirmed the ultimate mysteriousness of reality, challenging science's hegemony on certainty. Modern physics tells us quite calmly that light is both a particle and a wave, a paradox quite incomprehensible and devastating to the human mind. The brilliant mathematician Kurt Gödel, known for Gödel's Proof, has demonstrated that even mathematics does not provide absolute certainty. In 1933, as a young man of only twenty-seven, he confirmed that two quite different answers could be obtained from the same group of mathematical data. If mathematics could not lay claim to absolute certainty, as Gödel claimed, surely people must remain open to truth, whatever its source.

Aldous Huxley, the English novelist and philosopher, perhaps best known for his dystopian novel *Brave New World* (1932), moved to California in the late 1930s. In 1970, after experimenting with the mind-expanding drug mescaline, he reflected upon his experience in a short book, *Doors of Perception*. He concluded that human beings are open to a vast array of experiences, many of which are forgotten, overlooked, or go unnoticed because the function of the brain and nervous system is to protect us from being overwhelmed and confused by this large mass of knowledge, much of it useless and irrelevant. This leaves only a small and special selection that may have practical value, including the practices of spirituality, conscious and unconscious, described at length by William James in *The Varieties of Religious Experience* and by Morton Kelsey in *Companions on the Inner Way*. (For a listing and discussion of Kelsey's thirty-six ways by which humans can relate to the divine, see chapter 4 below.) Human insight, imagination, and intuition supply convincing evidence of the pervasive and comprehensive spiritual nature of the universe, including seemingly unlimited opportunities for experiencing the sacred.

---

3. Rohr, *Falling Upward*, 157.

As Huxley suggests, many human beings rest content with the meager trickle of experience that remains after the total possibilities of experience have been funneled through the "reducing valve" of our brain, sense organs, and nervous system. The problem is compounded when we try to express this reduced awareness of the universe through language. Language and writing provide access to other people's experience, but they can also limit our view of reality by confirming the idea that this reduced awareness is the only experience available. Furthermore, humans frequently get in the habit of confusing concepts for data and words for actual things.

Over time, different cultures have developed many words for things that are important to them and few words for what they consider unimportant or "nonexistent" aspects of reality. Eskimos, for example, have a great many words to describe different kinds of snow. Greeks have five words for "love" and twelve different words to describe encounter with nonphysical dimensions of reality. Hindus have over twenty words that describe various aspects of spiritual experience, but few words to deal with different aspects of the physical universe. By contrast, the English language has only one vague and much abused word to describe human encounter with the spiritual realm, the term "mysticism." Something is surely wrong with our religious imagination, if not with our spirituality. In the language of Western culture, the supernatural realm has surely suffered from reduced awareness. If this reductionist trend in the Western religious sensibility continues, we will become a nation of spiritual orphans.

Thankfully, modern thinking is making room for spirituality, disclosing ways by which we can open up our capacities of knowing and coming into contact with contrasting realms of experience available to us. Those who would use reason to argue God out of experience no longer have precedence over than those who use reason to argue God into reality.

Having examined the limitations of various modern forms of disbelief, is there an alternative? I believe there is, and that it has been in the West all along. The alternative is found in the writings and beliefs of Plato; the Hebrew prophets; Jesus; early Christian thinkers such as Origen, Athanasius, and Augustine; medieval monastics and mystics such as Bernard of Clairvaux, Francis of Assisi, Julian of Norwich, Catherine of Siena, Catherine of Genoa, and Bonaventure; the Spanish mystics Teresa of Avila and John of the Cross; reformers such as Martin Luther, John Calvin, and Ignatius Loyola; revivalists such as Jonathan Edwards, John Wesley, and George Whitfield; and more recently William James, Carl Jung, and philosophers of science such as Heisenberg and T. S. Kuhn. To find it, however, we must use our imagination and insight, thereby breaking with the materialistic presuppositions of the last thousand years of Western thought. This way will confirm that what we experience spiritually is real, however partial and imperfect our understanding and comprehension.

Our knowledge of reality and our experience of its underlying spiritual essence can grow if we observe and adopt the methodology developed by the physical sciences. This approach, essential to science, is called the inductive method (despite combining induction with deduction). This method follows a four-step process, beginning with the painstaking process of observation and comparison of the data on the subject under consideration, in our case, the subject of spiritual experience. This initial step is followed by a second, whereby one arrives at a hypothesis regarding how and why the data are relevant. Significantly, this process is guided less by reason than by intuition and imagination. Paul Feyerabend, a respected philosopher of science, suggests that if society wishes to produce creative scientists, the development of their imagination is of greater importance than the development of their purely logical and rational capacities. Once a hypothesis is framed, we use our best powers of rational analysis and deduction to sketch out the implications of our theory. If some of the data of experience do not agree with the theory that has been formulated, and these continue to appear, then a new hypothesis is required, and the whole process begins anew. A new hypothesis is imagined, which is then subjected to further testing, and so the process of understanding continues.

Human beings have the capacity to see beyond the appearance of things and grasp their essence. Plato spoke of a mathematical intuition by which humans perceive the structure of reality. It was through this kind of insight that Isaac Newton constructed his monumental vision of the order with the cosmos. Kurt Gödel spoke of the insight through which mathematicians perceive the truths of their discipline and compared this to how Plato believed humans encounter eternal forms and essence (called Ideas or Ideals). Such "seeing through" ordinary reality, if carried far enough, can bring religious observers to a religious understanding of reality, though with obvious limitations.

Young children live comfortably between two worlds. It takes years of training in our materialistic culture to persuade them that only the physical world is real. Children tend not to distinguish between outer and inner reality; their imagination is for them as real as hard physical reality. There are few better descriptions of this aspect of childhood than Frances Wickes's *The Inner World of Childhood*. The poet William Blake was beaten because he insisted he saw spirits in the streams and trees, and although he learned to distinguish the external from the internal, he never gave up his inner vision. Hallucination occurs when we attribute to the outer world what has come to us only through the inner one. A sound ego helps us from being overwhelmed by the contents of the unconscious psyche.

Fantasy literature, such as the popular novels of J. R. R. Tolkien or the children's stories of C. S. Lewis, has long ushered adults and children alike across the boundaries of the purely physical realm, fostering real encounters with other dimensions. Likewise, religious ritual uses poetry, incense, stained glass windows, architecture, music, sculpture, painting, dance, and storytelling to expand human horizons and provide a taste of the divine. Greek and Russian Orthodox Christians have long used icons as windows into heaven. Great music, drama, and literature have long transported believers beyond the limits of a purely materialistic world.

Artistic inspiration is one of the most important natural ways by which we receive glimpses of the spiritual world and its importance. With few exceptions, nearly every religion uses artistic expressions to mediate their experience of the divine source of life. In fact, most religious rituals have their root in dramatic reenactment, reliving sacred events so that devotees can participate in them. The Christian Eucharist allows believers to step by divine play into the drama of redemption. Like all great drama, religious rituals enable human beings to step into another world, introducing us to a deeper dimension of life.

Related to imagination is our capacity for intuition, the perception of meanings and realities other than those perceived through the five senses. Jung, in his important distinction between psychological types, suggested that we have two quite different ways of taking in data, one through the senses, which he called sensation, and another that he called intuition. Nearly all human beings have intuitions—hunches or vague flashes of understanding. All humans share this capacity. Those who develop this capacity most highly could call their ability insight. The Myers-Briggs Type Indicator, developed in conjunction with Jungian psychological typology, is a device that helps analysts determine how much their clients prefer to use their capacity for intuition. Through intuition, human beings sometimes learn about physical and nonphysical realities within or beyond their psyches.

Questions for Discussion and Reflection

1. Did you ever question God's existence? If so, how old were you? Do you remember how it felt? Did you share this experience with anyone?
2. Do you believe God's existence can be proven? If so, how?
3. If your belief in God is faith-based, how do you distinguish between reasoned faith and mere wish-fulfillment?
4. In your view of God, do you consider yourself a theist, an agnostic, an atheist, or something else? Explain your answer.
5. In your estimation, is there purpose to life? If so, what is it? How do you know?
6. At this moment, which stage of life most characterizes your spirituality: precritical understanding, critical understanding, or postcritical understanding? Explain your answer.
7. If modern society is abandoning traditional religion and its values, what is its loss? What attitudes and values guide nonreligious people today?
8. Is the church responsible—at least in part—for modern disbelief? Is there anything the church can do to reverse the tide of materialism, skepticism, and disbelief? Support your answer.
9. What does it mean to characterize our society as postmodern? How has modern science contributed to this mindset?
10. Assess the merits of the philosopher Immanuel Kant's view that knowledge of the noumenal world is both unknowable and unattainable to human beings? What knowledge did he have in mind? What are the results, psychologically and spiritually, of such a perspective?

CHAPTER 3

What Does It Mean to Experience God?

> God is an intelligible sphere, whose center is everywhere
> and whose circumference is nowhere.
>
> —ALAIN OF LILLE

IF THERE IS A world of spiritual reality, how do we get in touch with it? This is the subject of the next three chapters. This chapter contains a discussion of general aspects of the divine-human encounter. Chapter 4 explores the religious quest by examining the variety of specific religious experiences available to human beings, both spontaneous and those sought through religious practice, and chapter 5 introduces a specific method for experiencing God in everyday life.

Human Development, Relationships, and Transcendent Experience

When children are born, they are equipped with both a physiological and a psychic inheritance. In their first weeks and months, their most essential need, in addition to food and shelter, is bonding with other human beings, ideally the mother and father. One cannot overestimate the importance of physical closeness and touch for newborn infants. In foundling homes, where orphaned or abandoned children are cared for, in cases where children are left alone in cribs except for feeding, nearly a third died of marasmus. This disease, which causes children mysteriously to waste away, largely ceased when attendants were hired in these homes to hold the children and play with them, giving them human warmth and contact.

Children who have not experienced this kind of intimacy find it difficult to believe that there is any caring at the center of the universe. Friedrich von Hügel (1852–1925), one of the most original theologians of his era, suggests that Freud had it backward. Freud thought that human religious experience and longing is merely a wish to return to the womb, whereas for von Hügel this period of intense human closeness was designed by God so that we might be prepared to relate to the loving deity at the core of the universe.

The early period of closeness is followed by one in which children become aware of their own separateness and personal identity. They move away from their mother and begin to explore the world around them. They begin the development of an ego, a sense of autonomy and self-direction. During this period, there often emerges an imaginary playmate who has the same reality as the people of the outer world. Gradually, the child clearly distinguishes the physical world from the reality perceived through the inner world. During early childhood we learn a language in order to communicate with those around us and to find different levels of intimacy. Language provides an incredible tool for gaining knowledge and for exploring our world. Around the age of five, children become insatiable seekers after knowledge.

As we mature and widen our experience, we realize that our parents and teachers are fallible and that we need to form our own opinions and our own social setting. During adolescence we pass from childhood to adulthood. During this period we begin to separate out from parental values, to consider various professions, and to discover where our most compelling interests drive us. We begin to seek adult forms of intimacy, laying the foundation for two of the most important aspects of mature behavior: autonomy and the need for close relationships. Those who develop only one of these foundations of genuine maturity are cheated and stunted. These two qualities are like the two foci of an ellipse; human fulfillment requires both.

As adults we try to master the problem of living in our social group, relating intimately with other human beings, raising a family, and making it in the world. The importance of a strong sense of self and a healthy ego for this stage of life cannot be overstated.

Then, sometime around midlife, many adults—particularly those who have not known consistent affection and caring during childhood and who have developed powerful egos—experience a crisis. This midlife crisis can take many forms, including experiencing an overwhelming sense of meaninglessness or agonizing depression, becoming obsessed with anxiety or by compulsions and addictions they do not understand, and the loss of intimate relationships. At times physical illness appears as well.

In *The Varieties of Religious Experience*, William James makes a clear and important distinction between the "once-born" and the "twice-born." The once-born are those who have been integrated into a family and a culture with a sound religious foundation. They seldom go through a traumatic change in midlife. However, in our secular and materialistic culture, most men and many women must be "twice-born" somewhere between thirty-five and forty-five as they come to the sudden realization that life without transpersonal meaning is not worth living. Ordinary living in the world loses its meaning, and some or all of the above problems arise.

One of the goals of genuine education is keeping children open to the spiritual domain while at the same time helping them deal effectively and creatively with the physical world. We know how much training it takes to begin to understand the mysteries of the subatomic realm. Should we expect it to be simple to learn how to know and relate to the creative spiritual source of this material universe?

The physical world alone is value-free; no moral system satisfactory to any great number of people has been devised that does not incorporate some transcendental values. Those who have been brought up in and have assimilated the rational materialism of our culture need to be provided both an intellectual foundation that makes sense of non-material reality and a way to experience nonphysical reality.

Some people have spontaneous conversion experiences such as those described by William James; these people sometimes find meaning without understanding why, but such acceptance is often rigid and uncritical, and it is difficult to convey to others. Few educated Westerners can accept only authority as a basis of belief and practice, and reason alone seldom allows us to escape a reductionist materialistic perspective, a view that limits the universe to the physical realm.

Those individuals who pass through their midlife in relationship with the divine source of life often find that life takes on new meaning. Monumental change may take place in how they relate to spouse, children, relatives, friends, strangers, enemies, and to the poor, the oppressed, and forgotten. Such individuals begin to spend their time differently, use their money differently, and seek for a quality of love and experience that does not end in self-gratification.

This period of new awareness can become the most creative of life, when enhanced abilities, aided by healthy identities, can be directed in the service not just of ourselves but of others and of the divine. This is also a time to achieve inner harmony. As we detach from jobs and careers, we find release from tension, conflict, fear, despair, and anger that once prevented us from functioning in ways that are creative for ourselves and for those around us. As we learn to live in the Spirit, we discover we can influence others in profound and inexplicable ways, often without saying a word.

People that make a regular commitment each day to keep in close relationship with Spirit find restoration and new direction. Some feel called to minister to the poor; to take care of the dying; to advocate against war, violence, and injustice; to help the confused and depressed; and to stand up to prejudice. Spending time in meditation and prayer, writing, or drawing, they discover meanings and talents they can share with others. Of course, there are people who are called to this kind of reflection early in life, finding opportunities in contemplation, solitude, and prayer for expanded awareness and enhanced experiences of the divine.

Images of God

Children are taught certain things about the nature of God at an early age. Many of these teachings prove to be immensely helpful and provide a sound basis for later development, but many are also confusing and lead to distortion. For example, some parents use a God image to help maintain discipline and control. They portray God as a stern judge, a severe taskmaster who keeps an ongoing tally of the child's deeds and misdeeds. Other parents, perhaps in an attempt to prevent such harshness, present God as Love, thereby avoiding all anthropomorphism. For small children, this image may be too abstract to integrate in a meaningful way. While it preserves the mystery of God, it does not give children someone personal to whom they can pray or with whom to relate. The image of God as "Father," commonly used, is inevitably influenced by the child's human father, and thereby can restrict children's experiences in meditation, worship, and prayer.

Regardless of what images are presented by parents, most children develop a sense of God as being active in their lives. They see God as a person or force that influences their daily activities, bringing good things or abandoning them to bad things. In either case, they relate to God through appeasement, much as adults do when they are frightened or despairing.

At some point it becomes clear that images of God are not God. As people mature and grow spiritually, some images of God die and are replaced by others, while some images remain deep within, unchanging yet affecting human experience.

Revivals and Awakenings

It should come as no surprise to learn that spiritual hunger is decreasing for many in our current American culture. What a change from the 1960s and 1970s, a time described by William McLoughlin as a Fourth Awakening in American history.[1] During this period millions of Americans participated actively in spirituality, many experimenting with Transcendental Meditation, various forms of yoga, and other forms of Eastern religion. In addition, millions of Christians were involved in the charismatic movement and in related aspects of Pentecostal spirituality. Many others sought to expand their spiritual awareness through the use of hallucinogens and other mind-expanding drugs. In 1975, a survey by sociologist Andrew Greeley revealed that close to 40 percent of his sample indicated they had had a mystical experience, one that followed the fourfold criteria of such experience formulated by William James in his classic study *The Varieties of Religious Experience* (first published in 1902).[2] By "mystical" James spoke of visionary, revelatory, unitive, transcendental, or trance-like states of consciousness characterized by four qualities, namely, ineffability (a state of feeling that defies expression), noetic quality (a state of knowledge with a definite cognitive dimension), transiency (the experience is short-lived), and passivity (the experience is involuntary in nature).[3]

McLoughlin characterized his Fourth Awakening as a "Romantic" awakening of experiential, quest-oriented, and self-aware religion. This emerging spirituality was grounded in a new social vision, for it included a profound commitment to justice, pluralism, freedom, and inclusive democracy. Other analysts dubbed this movement the "Next Christendom," claiming that America was witnessing the most significant change in the Christian faith since the Protestant Reformation. Traditional Christians watched from the sidelines, perplexed at the unfolding drama of this paradigm shift.

During previous "awakenings" in American history—the first (c. 1730–1760) in the years before the American Revolution; the second (c.

1. McLoughlin, *Revivals, Awakenings, and Reform.*
2. Greeley, *Sociology of the Paranormal.*
3. James, *Varieties of Religious Experience*, 267–268.

1800–1830) in the early decades of the American republic; and the third (1890—1920) as the United States became an industrial world power—religious, political, social, and cultural values and institutions underwent profound change, as people searched for deeper understandings of selfhood, meaning, and purpose in the world.

McLoughlin speculated that 1978, the year his book was published, marked the halfway point in the process of revitalization, anticipating that a consensus would emerge in the early 1990s that would result in a fundamental spiritual restructuring of American life and institutions. The transformation he anticipated did take place, but it was technological rather than spiritual in nature. During the 1980s, two changes occurred that profoundly changed American society: the Reagan presidency, which led to a new sense of security, due to the end of the Cold War and a nostalgic wave that swept the nation, and the implementation of nanotechnology, which produced cell phone and social networking and led to the wonders—and dangers—of the digital age. Americans, benefiting from the omniscience of the Internet and riding a wave of instant interconnectivity, were experiencing new powers as science led the way toward a utopian kingdom on earth. The Fourth Great Awakening, unable to sustain momentum, came to an abrupt halt.

The results, as described by *The Huffington Post*'s Diana Butler Bass, include "a generative spirit, a creative and innovative openness, a sense of hope-filled realism, of pragmatic idealism, of an interconnectedness of all things, of urgency and wonder, and of experiencing the divine in the here and now."[4] In 2016, the *Gallup Poll on Religion in America* revealed continuing disturbing trends in religion. Among the findings was that while the United States remains a largely Christian nation, close to 20 percent of Americans now say they no longer identify with a specific religious group. Since the early 2000s, the United States had seen an increase in those with no formal religious identity (called "nones"), a figure that had increased dramatically since the 1950s and 1960s. Another alarming trend was a decrease in attendance of organized worship, a figure that had plummeted consistently since the final decades of the twentieth century and continued its plunge at the start of the twenty-first century. For example, during 2014–2016, only 36 percent of respondents claimed to attend church regularly, a significant drop since the mid-twentieth century.

Interestingly, a majority of Americans still say that religion is "very important" in their lives, despite their claims that organized religion is losing

---

4. Bass, *Christianity After Religion*, 247.

its influence in society. Also significant is the high percentage of Americans that claim to believe in God. About eight in ten Americans say they believe in God or in a universal spirit (one in ten Americans report they are "not sure" and one in ten reports "no belief" in God). Though belief in God is down in past decades, it has not dropped as precipitously as belief in angels, heaven, hell, or in a personal devil. Despite all else, Americans are unwilling to give up on God!

Eastern Spirituality

During the 1960s and 1970s, one of the strangest aspects of the spiritual resurgence was the minimal effect it had on traditional Christian churches. Traditional churchgoers, it seems, were more interested in maintaining institutional status quo than experiencing mind alteration. The spiritual paradigm shift of the Fourth Awakening simply bypassed traditional Christianity. It flourished, however, in the emergence of new charismatic churches that introduced the New Testament gifts of the Spirit into public and private worship. The failure of traditional churches to adopt these new spiritual interests and concerns also led to an exodus of many Christians, primarily adolescents and young adults, away from the church. Many turned instead to the rich tradition of Eastern religions such as Hinduism and Buddhism, which displayed a deep understanding of the human psyche and which had a profound heritage for dealing with the spiritual world.

There was a problem, however, for those spiritually hungry Westerners who plunged into Eastern traditions. While Eastern religions provided helpful devotional practices, these practices were based on a view of reality diametrically opposed to the materialistic perspective dominant in modern America. Hinduism and Buddhism view the outer, physical world as illusion (*maya*). Human emotions, byproducts of conscious participation in that world, are viewed as distractions from the spiritual goal, meaning they should be suppressed, overcome, and eliminated. The goal of life is not fullness and abundance, as in the West. Rather the goal of spirituality is to render humans passionless, emotionless. To achieve this end, love, pity, anxiety, anger, desire, and self-concern are to be rooted out. Concern for specific human being in their sickness, tragedy, or grief, while endorsed, has limited value, for these too are illusions. To help others in need might actually interfere with the karmic value of their suffering. Thus, there is little emphasis on acts of kindness or charity in Eastern religions. All people are getting exactly what they deserve.

The distinction between subject and object is also viewed as illusion in the East, since all reality is psychic in nature. This understanding of reality expresses a perspective vastly different from that of Western materialism. The critical scientific attitude that emerges from serious analytical study of the physical world is almost unknown in cultures that treat this reality as *maya*.

Since Eastern religions view the life process as essentially cyclical, reincarnation is the way the soul grows and matures as it passes from one life cycle to another. How one lives and thinks in this life merely augments or detracts from this seemingly endless cycle of rebirth. In reality, this perspective minimizes the intentions and accomplishments of one's life. What we think and how we live have only temporary relevance, not eternal consequences, for opportunities lie ahead, in future lives, for change and correction.

Unfortunately, few people today realize that there is any reasonable alternative to the Eastern and Western understandings of the universe. Either the physical world is seen as real and the human soul is an illusion—in which case all spiritual striving is vain or folly—or else the physical world is an illusion and concern with it leads away from salvation. There is, however, a third view of the world. It is widespread and has been accepted in many times and places. This third view of reality was accepted by Greek philosophers such as Plato, by many of the Hebrew prophets, and was the way Jesus of Nazareth viewed this universe. This view proposes that both the physical world and the spiritual world are real. Human beings need to participate in both of these worlds if they are to be fully alive.

This point of view undergirded the thinking of early Christianity, which combined the insights of Plato and the teachings and practices of Jesus. The great church fathers, including Origen, Athanasius, and Augustine, hammered out Christian dogma using the same base. This perspective gave rise to a rich and lively devotional practice, which animated the early church and continued through medieval times. This religious practice was gathered and systematized by Ignatius of Loyola between 1522 and 1524 in his *Spiritual Exercises*. His approach followed the kataphatic tradition of prayer, a meditational form of prayer that uses images in devotional practice to mediate the divine.

As noted above, during the spiritual awakening of the 1960s and 1970s many Westerners, including denominational and nondenominational Christians, turned to the East rather than to the spiritual tradition of Western Christianity. They did so for many reasons. In part they were looking for something different, something exotic, and the presence of numerous Hindu gurus, newly admitted to the United States and anxious to proselytize, made their customs, practices, and perspectives increasingly attractive. The failure of traditional American churches was also a factor, whether due to disinterest in the ongoing cultural revolution or to ignorance of the rich spiritual tradition of the West.

The classical Christian view of reality, which was never lost in the Greek Orthodox tradition, had been largely supplanted in Europe during late medieval times by the philosophy of Aristotle. Within this philosophical system human beings have no direct contact with a spiritual world. Humans are limited to experiences of the five senses with which to explore the knowable world and with reason to make logical deductions and inferences about that part of the world we cannot experience through the senses. Unlike his teacher Plato, Aristotle cast grave doubts upon the existence of any world not discovered by reason and sense experience.

The beliefs of Aristotle came to be foundational for both Protestant and Catholic scholasticism. In the eighteenth and nineteenth centuries the rich and lively devotional practice that animated the early church and continued through medieval times was largely lost. During the same period the secular world became increasingly satisfied with rational materialism. Many Enlightenment thinkers followed the lead of Thomas Hobbes, who denied the existence of any spiritual world. In the nineteenth century, chemistry, physics, medicine, and other sciences produced dramatic successes without taking any spiritual dimension into consideration. Many thinkers concluded that science had final truth and the spiritual world was illusory. Scientific inquiry, it seems, had solved most problems and had left only a few untidy ends to tie together to complete its perfect understanding. William James refers to this pervasive point of view as rationalism and points to its inadequacy in *The Varieties of Religious Experience*.

Our Primal Ancestors

Spirituality is universal and timeless. The first humans—our earliest ancestors—were deeply spiritual, and human beings have been spiritual ever since.

While we sometimes tend to think of the first humans as primitive—they were certainly primitive technologically—it is better to call them primal, for they came first, and their worldview was more sophisticated than that of many moderns. Everything for them was religious, for they thought of nature as imbued with sanctity. Furthermore, they viewed life and nature with wonder and reverence, for they envisioned no line separating the visible world from the more real spiritual world that surrounded and nurtured the physical realm. Primal peoples were concerned (and continue doing so, for their holistic views are perpetuated in primal societies still found across the globe, such as in Native American groups and societies found throughout North and South America) with the maintenance of personal, social, and cosmic harmony, because for them all things were related.

Primal people are embedded in their world. Their rituals are not attempts to stand apart from or to control nature, for primal people view humanity and nature as belonging to a single order. Rather than attempting to produce extraordinary effects or control nature magically, primal rites focus on maintaining the patterns on nature; they are rituals of cooperation rather than of coercion or manipulation. While articulating basic human needs, these rituals also sustain confidence in the processes of nature, spiritually conceived, and renew hope for the future.

Primal people view animals and plants as "spirit guides," both because they preceded human being in antiquity and because they are believed to have a spiritual nature, like humans. Primal people are not blind to nature's differences, for they are known for their powers of discernment and observation. However, they see distinctions in nature as bridges rather than as barriers to religious experience, for all things are alive, interdependent, and interrelated. Significantly, the overriding goal of salvation (meaning release from this world to a vastly different and unrelated realm) that dominates historical religions is virtually nonexistent in primal cultures, and life after death tends to be vague and shadowy. Life in the present is central and primary, and cosmic relatedness is a reality to be cultivated here and now. While nonprimal people like ourselves welcome scientific and technological progress as valuable, and promote the gains of such advancement, in our rush forward we need to recover what we have relinquished spiritually.

IN THE POTTER'S WORKSHOP

The Western Christian Spiritual Tradition

Religious practice is common the world over, a natural way for human beings to remain open to the wider world of spiritual experience. Nevertheless, to cultivate our experience of God, we need not look to other traditions or search for exotic non-Christian ways to experience the holy. For that we need only become acquainted with the richness of the Western Christian spiritual tradition.

The spirituality of the West arises out of the Western worldview, with its distinct perspective. How one views spiritual reality, particularly its core or center, influences religious practices and outcomes. For example, worship of the warlike Norse god Wotan can produce Hitler and Nazism, whereas worship of a loving Christ can produce Francis of Assisi and Mother Teresa. Furthermore, how one envisions the goal of the faith journey will shape that person's experience of God. In this respect, the psychotic who denies the reality of the physical world and dwells almost exclusively in the inner or psychoid dimension of life is not far worse than the consistent materialist, who by denying the existence of the spiritual world dwells exclusively in the physical realm. The mature adult who chooses to live in both realms simultaneously is far healthier for doing so.

However, if the goal of the religious adult is simply experience, bliss, or a flight away from physical reality with its challenges and responsibilities, the results may lead not only to pride and egomania, but to psychoses as well. In *Care of the Soul*, psychotherapist Thomas Moore indicates that a spiritual life of some kind is necessary for psychological health, but he cautions that excessive or ungrounded spirituality can be dangerous, leading to compulsive and even violent behavior.[5] It is far better for religious seekers to embrace a historical religion, one in which religious practices have been tested and refined over time, than to experiment solo or by joining some new sect that pretends to have a new revelation of final truth. There is, however, an equally great and grave danger when people blindly accept the practices, methods, and beliefs of any established religion, for religious practices and beliefs that are not tested by individual experience or subjected to criticism and change can degenerate into bigotry and brainwashing. A wise therapist once noted that brainwashing occurs whenever someone is made to feel guilty for doubt.

---

5. Moore, *Care of the Soul*, xii–xiii.

WHAT DOES IT MEAN TO EXPERIENCE GOD?

The spirituality of the West arises out of the Christian worldview, which affirms both the physical and spiritual realms as real, valuable, and interrelated. As sense experience and sense images connect us with a real physical world, so inner images can connect us with a real spiritual, metaphysical, realm. We need to develop sensitivity, awareness, and a capacity for critical thinking in order to deal with each realm. If we accept sense experience uncritically, we can fall into all sorts of delusion, such as the flatness of the earth, the rising and setting of the sun, and the earth as the center of the universe. Likewise, if we take images from dreams and visions or religious symbols and teachings as ultimate and final representations of reality, we can fall into similar absurdity.

Western spirituality regularly views the motivating and creative core of the universe as Divine Love. This is true of institutional and mystical Christianity. However, there is a vast difference between being absorbed into the cosmic One (such unity is the goal of much of Christian apophatic prayer and of many Eastern mystical traditions) and encountering Divine Love, which is the goal of Christian kataphatic prayer. Unfortunately, some writers on spirituality such as Jacob Boehme, Meister Eckhart, Thomas Traherne, and Matthew Fox, and poets and "nature mystics" such as Byron, Wordsworth, Blake, Emerson, Thoreau, Whitman, and Annie Dillard attempt to rescue mysticism and direct spiritual experience by describing spirituality as an ecstatic experience of the physical world. By so doing, they stop short of the experience we seek in this study, namely, intimacy with the personal God of the Christian tradition.

East and West offer similar disciplines for the beginning of the spiritual quest. Both emphasize detachment, quiet, stilling the emotions, withdrawal, receptivity, listening, and ceasing ego activity and striving. The reason is clear: if we are to find the spiritual realm and its central meaning in God, we need to detach ourselves from *exclusive* preoccupation with the physical realm

At this point, the spiritual understanding of the West diverges from that of the East. The Eastern way plunges into the depths of detachment and imagelessness, seeking extinction of the subject-object duality and individual consciousness. For the Western spirituality we are describing, once detachment has been achieved, the individual is redirected back to attachment, in this case to human love, compassion, and all the positive activity associated with beauty, goodness, and healthy vitality that accompany attachment to the Divine Lover. Here one relies on a host of images and symbols, natural and supernatural, that enable individuals to achieve greater wholeness and integration of their complex inner selves. Such integration, according to Western masters of spirituality, leads the individual into a relationship with the Divine Lover, which results in the transformation of the individual into the likeness of that to which he or she relates and beholds.

It is very difficult for human beings to be satisfied with a goal of life that contains two distinct elements, a goal that is not simple and straightforward. For an increasing number of modernist people, the possibility that humans can experience elements from both a physical and a nonphysical dimension of reality seems unrealistic and contrived. However, as modern physics indicates, light is both a particle and a wave, and even though most humans cannot comprehend such a paradox, they accept it as somehow real. As Heisenberg notes, these descriptions of light, while paradoxical, are complementary. Likewise, detachment and attachment are two aspects of the spiritual journey and the spiritual goal. Both are necessary if we would understand the nature of the spiritual journey.

It is nearly impossible to come to full development on the inner way without guidance. In addition to the experience of history and tradition, we also need training in critical thinking, in spiritual practices and disciplines, in the nature of the human psyche, and in the art of loving. We shall examine these areas in more detail in this study, guided by the following eight principles:[6]

- The physical realm is valuable in itself. There is no sharp division between the secular and religious, the physical and the spiritual; all are part of God's world.

- Each human being is unique and valuable to the Divine Lover. Those who experience God need to mediate God's love to all they meet. How we treat others, we treat God. And as we love others, we often find the divine within those we love.

- Physical science, when it is free of reductionist bias, complements healthy spirituality. The seeker need fear no truth. The objectivity that genuine scientific study provides can greatly help overcome superstition, prejudice, and uncritical sentimentality.

- The growth potential of the human being is infinite. Hope for an extension of life beyond the grave contributes to a healthier and more

---

6. These principles are adapted from Kelsey, *Companions on the Inner Way*, 25–28.

productive life. However, this hope should not detract from commitment to this life and to the fullness of joy that is possible for those who live each day lovingly and responsibly.

- To achieve our full potential we must continuously be more loving and compassionate, using all methods at our disposal. Since growth and transformation are given, not earned or achieved, a simple childlike trust is as valuable as wisdom and spiritual practice.

- A Christian meditative practice that does not result in horizontal outreach to suffering human beings has gone astray. The more deeply we encounter the Divine Lover, the more sensitive we become to the pain of the world. Evil exists in both the outer and inner worlds, but it can be overcome by Christ's way of conquering, namely, with love.

- Our knowledge and understanding of God can increase as long as we live. As our knowledge of this physical world is imperfect, our knowledge and experience of God are imperfect. In our spiritual journey, we should use the best Christian traditions available, testing them by our own experience in prayer, meditation, and contemplation. We need to apply all our abilities—physical, intellectual, and emotional—in our pursuit of God.

- Our religious practice should result in spiritual, emotional, and intellectual maturity as well as in improved physical and psychological wellbeing.

Questions for Discussion and Reflection

1. What is your earliest memory or thought about God? How old were you? Where were you? Do you remember how you felt? Did you share this experience with anyone?

2. How did you think or perceive of God when you were in elementary school? In your early teenage years? In your high school years? As a young adult? Has anything changed about your concept of God? What are these changes, and when did they begin to occur?

3. When was the last time you remember feeling especially close to God? Where were you? Do you remember how you felt? Did you share this experience with anyone?

4. Using William James's terminology, do you consider yourself "once-born" or "twice-born"? Explain your answer. Have you ever had a "conversion" experience? Where were you? Do you remember how your felt? What difference did it make in your life? Explain your answer.

5. Were you alive during the 1960s? From your knowledge or awareness of this period, would you characterize it as a time of spiritual awakening? Explain your answer.

6. How would you explain the current drop in church attendance? In your estimation, is this an alarming trend? If organized religion is losing its influence in society, should Christians work to restore that influence?

7. Is the era of church and Sunday School waning? If so, what will replace it?

8. In your estimation, should Christians wishing to deepen their spiritual awareness experiment with Zen, yoga, and other Eastern meditational traditions? What is gained and what is lost by such excursions?

9. In your estimation, is reincarnation a valid alternative to the Christian belief in an afterlife or in rewards and punishments? Explain your answer.

10. What, to you, are the principal flaws in rationalism and materialism? How does the Western Christian spiritual tradition address those flaws?

11. Of the eight principles listed at the end of this chapter, does one stand out above the rest in priority or importance? Explain your answer.

CHAPTER 4

Varieties of Religious Experience

> We live in a sacramental universe.
>
> —MORTON T. KELSEY

AS WE LEARN FROM the vast literature on spirituality, there is a rich and varied tapestry of religious experience, many ways by which we can be opened to the whole world of spirit. A good place to begin is with Paul's discussion of the gifts of the Spirit in 1 Corinthians 12. In his letter, Paul commends the Corinthian believers for their interest in the realm of the Spirit, but as he notes, this interest has led to much dissension in the congregation, dividing the believers into competing groups and promoting self-aggrandizement, displayed by the motto, "my spirituality is better than yours."

In 1 Corinthians 12:8–10 Paul lists nine gifts given by God's Spirit as evidence that the spiritual realm is close at hand and is constantly flowing into human life. Spiritual gifts were admired in Paul's churches and widely manifest in his time. What prompted Paul's teaching about spiritual gifts in his letters was not their legitimacy but their misuse.

Paul uses various Greek terms to convey the idea that life in Christ is empowered by the Holy Spirit, often *pneumatika* (think of the English word "pneumatic," a reference to air or spirit), which emphasizes the spiritual origin of the gifts (*pneuma* means Spirit; see 1 Cor. 14:1), and also *charismata* (think of the English word "charismatic," a reference to spiritual power or extraordinary personality), which emphasizes that gifts are bestowed as an act of divine grace (*charis* means "grace").

As the body has many members, each with different functions, so the church is diverse, ethnically, socially, culturally, sexually, linguistically, theologically, and geographically. Paul celebrates this diversity as evidence of the Spirit at work. If all Christians are guided by the Spirit, he reasons, and if it is God's will that harmony and peace should be the hallmarks of the church (1 Cor. 14:33), then God will not only equip Christians for different ministries, but will also give others the grace to recognize and accept such Spirit-led leadership where it emerges.

Paul's premise is that God gives to every believer a spiritual ability to perform for the common good, to encourage and build up the church, which he calls the body of Christ. The *charismata* can be divided into three groups:

- Declarative gifts (power of speaking). Gifts of communication include prophecy, the ability to distinguish between true and false prophecy, speaking in tongues, and the ability to interpret speaking in tongues.
- Dynamic gifts (power of doing). Gifts of practical ministry include faith (the precondition for miracles), healing, and miracles.
- Discerning gifts (power of knowing). Pedagogical gifts include wisdom and knowledge.

In the letters of undisputed Pauline authorship, there are four separate listings of spiritual gifts: Romans 12:6–8; 1 Corinthians 12:8–10; 12:28; and 12:29–30. Since no lists are identical, they are suggestive rather than definitive. The simple imagery Paul uses in speaking of spiritual gifts introduces four decisive aspects of his thinking on the church and its members:

- All members are indispensable
- All members are different
- All members are equal
- All members are responsible

There is no question that people in biblical times were gifted with extraordinary abilities. Some of the gifts described in 1 Corinthians 12 appear to be heightened natural abilities, but some seem to be gifts of new and fresh insight. This emphasis gave urgency and vitality to the life of the early church. The Pentecostal movement, a fast-growing phenomenon in the twentieth century, which led to the establishment of several major denominations in the United States, also laid great importance on these particular gifts. Despite introducing anti-intellectualism and superstitious enthusiasm, the movement brought many to a renewed sense of Christian profession and practice. We will include these gifts in our discussion of the nature and variety of religious experience.

The religious experiences found below represents a simplification of Morton Kelsey's list of thirty-six ways by which humans connect with the divine.[1] Kelsey, an influential theologian during the second half of the twentieth century, was also a psychologist, educator, counselor, therapist, minster, and author. Kelsey's work, written with clarity and deep conviction, represents a lifetime of study devoted to the topic, and I can think of no one more experienced to guide us in this segment.

Although religious experiences are hard to classify, in part because some clearly overlap, Kelsey divides them into five broad categories.

1. *Spontaneous religious experiences.* Such experiences, said to come unsought and sometimes undesired, can produce a life change for the one who experiences them. The apostle Paul and Francis of Assisi are classic examples. These experiences, generally "visionary" or mystical in nature, are said to be characterized by four qualities: they are (a) ineffable (essentially indescribable), (b) noetic (they represent states of knowledge), (c) transient (short-lived), and (d) passive by nature (not achieved through human effort).[2] To these characteristics we add two qualities of the holy described by Rudolf Otto in his influential study, *The Idea of the Holy*. The holy is *fascinans*, meaning that it exerts an irresistible attraction because it is recognized as profoundly familiar and essential to humanity. The experience of the sacred always involves wonder and fascination. The holy is also *mysterium tremendum*, meaning that it is awesome and fearsome, for that which we encounter is always more than we can handle. Otto suggested that religious experience relies upon a deep sense of the "numinous." This term, from the Latin *numen* (holy, sacred), expresses a natural human response to the experience of the sacred developed prior to rational and moral notions about it. In this respect we can consider numinous experiences as primal, that is, as going back to the very origins of humanity.

To this category Kelsey includes experiences of dazzling darkness or overpowering light; of ravishing divine love (where power is consummated in self-giving love); conversion experiences (described by William James as being saved from sin or negative powers by divine love); encounters with the deceased; near-death and "out-of-body" experiences; and encounters with "spirit guides," which often come through dreams, visions, automatic writing, or through the imagination. Most of the time, such encounters produce banal results, but sometimes entire religious systems are produced in this way. For example, the Qur'an is said to have

---

1. See Kelsey, *Companions on the Inner Way*, 84-125.

2. These qualities are introduced in chapter 3, in the segment on "Revivals and Awakenings."

been dictated to Muhammad in this way. Those who believe in reincarnation explain these encounters by relating them to the former lives of those who have such experiences.

Another explanation of such encounters is psychological in nature, viewing them as a product of the unconscious mind or, as Jung suggested, the result of the collective unconscious. By "collective unconscious" Jung had in mind archetypal images and experiences coming from all time and space and said to reside in the inexhaustible bank of the human unconscious. Those who are open to this data bank are susceptible to experiences of this kind.

2. *Natural experiences of nonphysical reality.* Experiences of this group illustrate that the boundary between the natural and the supernatural is far more permeable than we ordinarily think, and that the sacred (understood as the source of all things) is a presence interpenetrating all things. Having this view of reality helps explain many quite common and ordinary experiences, such as:

- ESP (extrasensory perception), including telepathy (thought transfer), clairvoyance, precognition (the experience of perceiving events before they occur), and psychokinesis (whereby energy is released and directed toward the restoration and healing of some diseased organism);
- powerful emotions such as fear, love, and anger, which can open people up to nonphysical dimensions of experience;
- dreams, which often transmit information from the personal unconscious, the collective unconscious, and possibly even communication from the divine realm. Dreams and dream interpretation are often an important part of counseling and therapy. Throughout church history many religious leaders believed that God speaks through dreams;
- art, drama, poetry, music, film, novels, and fantasy literature, which can transport spectators and participants alike to deeper dimensions of life and produce ecstatic experiences. Plato noted in the *Phaedrus* that humans experience the sacred through various forms of "madness," including art, prophecy and divination, cathartic madness (through which he believed healing occurs), and love;
- suffering, which can be a gateway to the divine (this topic will be explored in chapter 9);

- dance and constant rhythmic physical activity, such as the whirling dervishes of some Islamic groups, which perform dance movements until trance-like states occur. Such altered states of consciousness can provide euphoria and the sense of wellbeing produced by some mind-altering drugs;
- the capacity of wonder, a state of mind that keeps humans expectant and open to surprise and astonishment. This quality of openness is a prerequisite of all learning and is as essential in religious experience as in scientific discovery. When Jesus told his followers they needed to become as children in order to enter the kingdom of God, he undoubtedly had in mind the sense of wonder and openness possessed by children;
- human love, including falling in love and its expression in sexuality, which has an ecstatic quality. Long ago Plato saw love as a means whereby humans become open to the spiritual world. He described the various aspects of love in *The Symposium*. One of the participants in this event tells a myth explaining the reason for the relentless attraction of love. According to this explanation, human beings were once whole, having male and female qualities. Such humans became a threat to the gods, who reacted by splitting each whole human into one of two persons. Love, then, is the desire of each half to be reunited with its other half, thereby achieving a state of equilibrium and of wholeness. Such projection or transference is the Romeo and Juliet state of love, about which so many dramas are staged, so many novels written, and so much music composed. The classical Greeks called this aspect of love *eros*, and saw it as coming from the god of love, Eros.

The New Testament speaks of another kind of love, *agape*, the kind of self-giving love that is more concerned with the growth and development, the welfare and wholeness of the other person than it is in finding those qualities for itself. This is the word that speaks of God's love for human beings. In John's Gospel, Jesus tells his disciples that they are his followers when they love one another as he loved them. Those who adopt the attitude of *agape* no longer see or treat others as the world does, for what they can offer or to be kept at arm's length, as strangers and threats to one's security and wellbeing. When we can see the divine even in the worst of human beings, we can turn enemies into friends. This is a quiet ecstasy, in which we look at the world from God's perspective, and it has the quality of divine joy. Such a perspective is transformative, and it possesses the power to turn human beings into agents of powerful, practical change.

At this point we need to remember that religious experience is not the goal of the spiritual journey. Rather the goal is continuing transformation by a conquering love greater than we can imagine. The reality of the transformation is tested as we help others to live in accordance with and empowered by the love we have experienced.

3. *Experiences deliberately sought through religious practice.* This is a large category, and some of its examples overlap with spontaneous experiences. Because religious practice is so common universally, it may well be the most natural way to remain open to the dimension of spiritual experience and to make contact with spiritual agents beyond the material world. While God or any other such agents, benevolent or malevolent, can invade our world and our experience with little or no conscious desire on our part, our participation in the sacred or divine realm begins when we consciously make an effort to relate to these powers.

While there are practically limitless practices through which people seek intimacy with or blessing from the divine, the following are common in our culture.

- *Sacramental acts or rituals.* Humans are sacramental creatures, and we regularly utilize common and life-sustaining elements such as bread and water to connect us with the divine. However, not all rituals are valid or equally useful. For example, while both the Eucharist and the Aztec human sacrifice stress the importance of sacrifice, one asks us to sacrifice voluntarily and inwardly and leads to new levels of living and giving of oneself to others, whereas the other sacrifices another person forcefully to placate the gods.

    While partaking a sacrament can produce salutary results, we need to refrain from dogmatic or exclusive attitudes, confusing the ritual or practice for the divine reality itself. When we think that only one form of observance is efficacious or correct, we debase religion and exhibit prejudice against those who do not practice or believe as we do, and we become bigots.

    Likewise, those who reject kataphatic aids as useless and favor only apophatic practices and beliefs can become equally dogmatic. The smashing of religious images common among certain radical religious groups, such as occurred during the Reformation, demonstrates ignorance and bigotry as well. A healthy psyche is a symbol-making psyche; even non-ritualistic Quakers have highly effective rituals of their own, such as the practice of silence, and this produces profound ability to listen for the divine voice within. Images and rituals carry a wealth of meaning and understanding, even for a specific religious tradition. The lack of institutional or communal tradition in a person's spiritual observance can produce a stunted outlook and can deeply thwart the horizontal outreach necessary for the display of love, compassion, and service to others.

Curiously, it was the Quaker author and teacher Richard Foster who wrote the best modern book on Christian spirituality and spiritual growth, a volume titled *Celebration of Discipline*. Foster divided his study into three broad categories including: (a) inward disciplines, comprising meditation, prayer, fasting, and study; (b) outward disciplines, comprising simplicity, solitude, submission, and service; and (c) corporate disciplines, comprising confession, worship, guidance, and celebration.

While Foster's approach focuses on the importance of discipline, the spiritual life also needs freedom and spontaneity, and an even more comprehensive catalog of religious practices than Foster provides.

- *Meditation and contemplation.* These techniques, central to the spiritual journey, include kataphatic and apophatic approaches to the experience of God.[3] Though some experts disagree, we will speak of meditation as sensate and verbal, as a process of quiet thinking and reflection that uses inner images, and of contemplation as silent and ineffable, as release from thought and image. In meditation, practitioners welcome thoughts and images that might arise. Whatever arises is important to the process; nothing is shut out or excluded. Because God's presence is in all thoughts and activities, seekers are asked to focus mindfully on the distractions, because in this case, nothing is distracting. In contemplation, practitioners focus on silence, gently setting aside distractions that arise. However defined, meditation and contemplation are complementary; neither is superior to the other.

In my experience, some form of meditation or contemplation is essential for personal growth and should accompany all other spiritual and devotional practices, not only for their health benefits but

---

3. Because these experiences are described at length in chapter 6, they are mentioned here for the sake of comprehensiveness.

also because without them it is nearly impossible to maintain regular and forward momentum in one's experience with God.

- *Visions and trance-like states.* In many cultures, revelation is given through the trance state. Mircea Eliade, the great Chicago historian of religion, wrote a definitive study of shamanism, showing how this phenomenon is found in nearly every human culture. There is an essential difference between the priest, who carries out rituals on behalf of an institution, and a shaman, who offers direct contact with the nomaterial dimension of reality for the specific benefit of the person seeking help. The Bible indicates that some of the great Hebrew prophets spoke out of trance-like states and had visions. They believed that this was a particular gift of God. In most societies, becoming a shaman requires a long period of training, and this is missing in many who dabble with this today.

- *Gifts of the Spirit.* We described these gifts, the *charismata*, earlier. The charismatic renewal of the twentieth century was considered visible evidence that the kingdom of God was exploding into the lives of ordinary Christians. Charismatic experiences should not be rejected, but rather interpreted within the context of a sound historical and liturgical tradition.

- *Divine healing.* The materialism of our age has silently eroded the healing practice that was central to Jesus' ministry and to patristic and medieval Christianity. If there is anything that can lift people out of the realm of disbelief and open them to the reality of God's presence today, it is being healed of illness. Healing is certainly possible through the Christian meditative practice, and a healing ministry can be an effective way to mediate the reality of the kingdom, as Paul indicates in Romans 15:18–19.

- *The use of oracles or related means to gain religious discernment.* Attempts to determine the will of God or the meaning of one's time and life have been used by nearly every developed religious group. Astrology, horoscopes, sacred tea leaves, the casting of sacred lots, the method of I Ching—the list is practically endless. Gideon used such a method in Old Testament times. The apostles did likewise when they chose the successor to Judas. Mennonite bishops are still selected that way, and most of us have opened a Bible at random and put our finger down on a verse to see if it can shed light on our situation. Somehow the depths of our being and the outer situation often produce hints of wisdom that we would not find otherwise.

- *Ascetic practices.* While asceticism has a bad connotation to most people, because it views the world, the body, and sex as evil in essence, the term has a helpful meaning. It comes from the Greek word meaning a discipline or an exercise that gives us greater proficiency in what we are doing. The popularity of Richard Foster's *The Celebration of Discipline* indicates the need we human beings have for discipline, for asceticism in this sense. There is also a need for freedom and spontaneity, and it is helpful to find disciplines in our life that can open us to the realm of the Spirit. Such discipline is what we are seeking through the practice of the presence of God.

- *Group process.* This category includes activities such as encounter groups, lengthy worship and prayer services, revival meetings, and evangelistic rallies. Many groups derive their power from group dynamics. Such gatherings can break down ego defenses and open participants to deeper levels of themselves or the spiritual world. When leaders of such groups are led by the Holy Spirit and love, the group can be remarkably creative. The fellowship of the early church surely had this spirit, as did the small groups of early Methodism and the revivals that often accompanied awakenings in America.

- *The monastic tradition.* While unique in its own way, the monastic tradition found in many religions provides opportunities for groups or individuals to express total dedication to the practice of faith. When the growing Christian movement accommodated to the secular and imperial world that finally accepted it, many pious individuals sought refuge in communities that emphasized dedication to the Christian life. While monastic life and religious orders allow devout believers opportunities for a lifetime of service and outreach, they are not always successful.

    Monasteries generally require celibacy, viewing sexuality as something that deters or prevents access to the fullness of God. These attitudes, however, are more reflective of the gnostic rejection of matter and the body than of authentic Christian belief. Some monastic communities have a more holistic approach, such as providing parallel living for men and women, so that they can meet at meals and work and pray together. There are even religious communities that allow married couples to live together in order that they might pursue prayer and service with greater devotion. Living in community enables people of certain psychological types to be more open to the spiritual dimension, but such situations are not suitable for everyone.

4. *Mental illness.* A fourth category of experience by which the spiritual or psychoid realm may intrude into human life is through mental illnesses such as neuroses and psychoses. In such instances there are imbalances between the conscious and the subconscious parts of the individual. Kelsey describes the differences between these in the following way: Neurotics understands reality but cannot accept it ("two and two is four and I can't stand it"), whereas psychotics accept as real their misunderstanding of reality ("two and two is twenty-two; isn't it wonderful?")

5. *Three Dangerous Doors.* Kelsey's final category includes experiences that are sought but which, unless well understood and protected with safeguards, can be quite dangerous. This category includes *hypnosis*, by which one person attempts to control another's personality or to change addictive behaviors such as smoking or overeating. When habits such as these are removed by hypnosis, some people actually experience deeper and darker problems.

Another dangerous practice, common in the history of religion, is the *use of mediums* to contact the dead or the nonmaterial realm. Such practice can lead to the loss of one's autonomy and can bring practitioners under the influence not only of evil spirits but also of powerful and dishonest individuals. C. S. Lewis once remarked that God has taken such trouble to keep the future from us that we would be wise to live in the present and leave the future to God.

A final danger is the use of *hallucinogenic drugs*, used by some to open themselves to the spiritual or psychoid dimension. The use of drugs within or outside well-developed religious traditions can be dangerous, particularly for people with personality disorders and weak self-control. Mild hallucinogens used regularly are also problematic, for they often lead to dissatisfaction with and withdrawal from the normal world. More potent hallucinogens can fling us into the depths of the unconscious, where there are both creative and destructive elements. Insight and mind-alteration may come by such means, but not likely from God's Holy Spirit.

VARIETIES OF RELIGIOUS EXPERIENCE

Questions for Discussion and Reflection

1. Are you familiar with the gifts of the Spirit listed in 1 Corinthians 12:8–10? Have you experienced any of these either directly or indirectly? If so, which? Are you comfortable or uneasy with spiritual gifts? Explain your answer.

2. In your estimation, what role should charismatic gifts play in one's spiritual journey with God? Is their value primarily individual or communal?

3. In your estimation, are some spiritual gifts more significant or desirable than others? If you were to ask God for a spiritual gift, which would you seek? Why?

4. Do you know anyone who is visionary, that is, who receives visions regularly? Have you ever had a visionary experience from God? If so, describe its content. Was it primarily for your edification or did it apply to others or to society as a whole?

5. Do you know anyone who has had an "out-of-body" experience? If so, give a brief description of this experience.

6. Do you or anyone you know have ESP or the ability of precognition? If so, describe the experience. Do you believe this ability is spiritual or merely psychological in nature? Explain your answer.

7. Do you consider dreams as vehicles of communication from God? Have you had any experience of this?

8. Have you ever felt the presence of God while participating in a sacramental ritual at church? If so, describe your experience. If not, why not?

9. Is there some aspect of church worship (such as music, scripture reading, prayer, silence, good preaching, or sacred space) that connects you with God? Explain your answer.

10. Have you or anyone you know ever experienced the spiritual dimension or God through hallucinogenic drugs? If so, describe the experience. In some societies, such as among Native Americans and Rastafarians, drugs are used sacramentally. How do you view such practice?

CHAPTER 5

Experiencing God in Everyday Life

*I cannot imagine how religious persons can live satisfied
without the practice of the presence of God.*

—Brother Lawrence

Christianity and most other major world religions teach us to focus on special times, persons, places, and things in life that they call "sacred." In this determination, they are correct: there are sacred times, persons, places, and things. However, by limiting the sacred in this way, they are also in error, for all times, persons, places, and things can be sacred.

As Paul indicates in his extended argument in 1 Corinthians on religious food laws and related practices, "All things are lawful, but not all things are beneficial" (1 Cor. 10:23). Eat whatever brings you benefit, he adds, and do not live in fear of religious retribution, for "the earth and its fullness are the Lord's" (1 Cor. 10:27–28). The overriding goal, found in 10:31, is clear: "So, whether you eat or drink, or whatever you do, do everything for the glory of God." As Paul indicates, all food and drink, like every circumstance in life, has sacramental value, if in our use of them and interaction with them God is glorified. In this respect, attitude and intent are all-important.

Do we see God in others? Do we eat ordinary food sacramentally? Do we acknowledge God's presence in each circumstance and situation of our everyday life, no matter how trivial? If so, these can become for us "thin places." The phrase "thin places," a metaphor taken from Celtic spirituality, refers to places, objects, events, persons, and other phenomena that are understood as being transparent to the divine. In "thin places" the boundary between the secular and the sacred, between the world of ordinary experience and the divine sense of all things, becomes diaphanous and permeable.

As I noted in my book *Into Thin Places*, "thin places are paradoxical: they are places of power and weakness; they provide weal and woe, bliss and pain; they are found in crosses and cancers but also in resurrection and remission; they may be ordinary, or extraordinary; sometimes they delight us, other times they perplex us . . . . Thin places fuel the imagination, foster risk-taking, feed the spirit, and foment human transformation. They have the ability to alter our way of thinking, transform our character, and renew our souls."[1] How can common things be so powerful and transformative? Because in them we affirm the presence of the sacred.

C. S. Lewis, one of the twentieth century's foremost Christian authors, knew about "thin places." He wrote about them in the *Chronicles of Narnia*, a set of seven children's classics in which he created a land of wonder and enchantment called Narnia. Following this publication, Lewis rigorously defended the fairy tale against those who claimed that it gives a false conception of life. Fairy tales, he argued, like myths, arouse longing for more ideal worlds while at the same time giving the real world a new depth. While Lewis's Narnia Chronicles remind us of other works, such as the Alice-in-Wonderland-like opening of *The Lion, the Witch and the Wardrobe* or the voyage of the *Dawn Treader*, which is akin to the voyage of Odysseus, Lewis blends Christian themes with events created from the rich world of fantasy. A dominant idea in his stories is that of an earlier time when reality was more harmonious and unified. It was Lewis's hope that upon reading these stories, children (and adults) would return to the "real world" with a new perspective, their minds opened to the possibilities of an unseen spiritual world and to the limits of merely human intellect and undeveloped imagination.

Lewis was referring to "thin places" without using the term. He knew, as children of all ages discover when they read his Narnia Chronicles or J. K. Rowling's Harry Potter books, that our world is alive with liminalities (threshold spaces between the sacred and the mundane); pictures, closets, fireplaces, train stations—any object, event, or person can open our minds to the possibilities and transport us to an unseen spiritual world.

Two Ways to Engage the Spiritual World

There are two quite different ways to enact or engage in the spiritual journey, often viewed as opposed to one another. The first is the sacramental method, in which the divine is mediated through words, images, pictures, symbols, and rituals. When this via positive, this way of affirmation, results

1. Vande Kappelle, *Into Thin Places*, xv–xvi.

in confusing the image or symbol with the reality, it can result in idolatry. Known as *the kataphatic way*, from the Greek meaning "with images," this indirect approach exemplifies much Christian practice.

The second approach, known as *the apophatic way*, from the Greek word meaning "without images," is based on the idea that one can best relate to the divine directly, apart from images and content. This via negative emphasizes the inadequacy of all images, descriptions, and pictures of the holy. Through silence, emptiness, and loss of self, this way of renunciation enables humans to experience the divine, abiding in it, achieving union with it, or losing themselves in it.

While both approaches are valid, depending upon the spirituality type and the needs of the seeker, neither approach guarantees authentic encounter. Of course we should all reject naïve kataphatic approaches, realizing that no symbol, image, or description contains all of an experience. On the other hand, we need to go beyond naïve apophatic approaches, so nebulous they fail to offer sufficient content. Both approaches are necessary and complementary parts of an adequate and informed spirituality. The apophatic emphasis, initially developed for the Christian monastic community, presupposes that in addition to silence and detachment, practitioners of this method would also attend the daily Eucharist and the offices of prayer, while also discharging the duties of study and service. Conversely, the kataphatic approach nearly always starts in silence and detachment before appropriating images. These approaches will guide our thinking throughout the remainder of this study. We will examine outer (kataphatic) spirituality in chapters 7, 8, and 10, and inner (apophatic) spirituality in chapters 6 and 8.

Practicing the Presence of God

While many practices we have mentioned, whether kataphatic and apophatic in nature, can enhance spiritual awareness, there is a third way, which need not end in failure or lead to divisiveness. More than a method, this approach to the sacred is an attitude that can be observed anytime and anywhere. Those who follow it will find it practical and effective because it is transformative and produces positive results, emotionally, spiritually, psychologically, and physically. It may be what Amy Carmichael had in mind when she wrote: "Let us die climbing; we would not tarry on the lower slopes," or what the psalmist envisioned when he declared: "This God—his way is perfect" (Ps. 18:30).

The attitude or way of life I have in mind was first described literarily by Brother Lawrence, an uneducated monk who joined the Carmelite order in Paris in 1666. As an eighteen-year-old, he saw a dry and leafless tree in midwinter, and the realization that it would blossom in full splendor in the spring triggered his conversion. He spent his long life devoted to simple tasks, finding in them opportunities to commune with God, constantly endeavoring to live as if he were in God's presence. The most common activities—eating, working in the kitchen, walking outdoors, meditating, worshipping—whether performed alone or in the company of others, became vehicles and opportunities to commune with God, audibly or silently.

Wishing to be guided by love, he resolved to make the love of God the goal of every thought and action. On occasion, while practicing a virtue or pursuing some endeavor, he addressed God directly, asking for requisite strength, insight, and ability. His impetus was similar to that of Paul, who spoke of receiving grace in time of weakness, and his perspective like that of the apostle, who spoke of being content with hardships and calamities, for when he was weak, then he was strong (2 Cor. 12:9–10).

Lawrence's lifestyle of faith taught him to distinguish between matters of understanding and those of the will, the first of relatively little value compared to the latter, which was supremely important. For Lawrence, the primary human concern should be to love God and delight oneself in God.

When outward duties and responsibilities distracted him from practicing the presence of God, he felt encouragement from God, which increased his passion and resolve. Surprisingly, he felt closer to God in mundane activities than while performing strictly devotional or religious duties. Such was his commitment to his goal that the worst that could happen to him would be to lose the sense of God's presence that so delighted him. When he was conscious of God's presence, he felt little fear or apprehension of danger, regularly finding sufficient guidance for his journey.

He became convinced that lack of advancement in the spiritual journey could be caused more by an excess of spiritual zeal than to not being spiritual enough. In other words, some people were too spiritual, meaning that they focused more on duties such as penance and related pursuits rather than on love and delight in God, which is their end. What a surprising thought, that it might be better to be less "spiritual" than too spiritual! Brother Lawrence felt he needed neither art nor science—meaning theological pedagogy or religious practice—to approach God, but only a heart determined to will one thing, to love God in each person he met and through every daily activity. Perhaps Jesus had this attitude in mind when he included "purity of heart" among the Beatitudes at the start of the Sermon on the Mount (Matt. 5:8). The blessing associated with that beatitude, you might recall, was that those who seek such purity would "see" God, not necessarily in the afterlife, or through participation in the sacrament, as we might assume, but in people around us as well as through the most common and mundane experiences of life.

If purity of heart means singularity of purpose, then those who dwell in the presence of God walk with the King. As Brother Lawrence notes, those who approach God with expectant hearts are not disappointed. They feel God's embrace, eat at God's table, and receive the very key to God's treasures. Lawrence likened his experience with God as one of mutual delight, as being God's favorite. At times, Lawrence considered himself as a stone before a sculptor. Presenting himself thus to God, he described his transformation as being made anew, as reflecting ever more perfectly God's image within. Whenever Brother Lawrence felt most unworthy of God's presence, whether due to sin or doubt, he felt more loved and accepted than before, and more united to God.

Can we acquire the mindset we have described, and maintain momentum? Can we experience the presence of God as did Brother Lawrence, both habitually and joyously? Such focus might not be possible to maintain in modern life, with its endless duties and distractions, but it is clearly impossible without singularity of purpose. Purity of heart starts with an act of our will. We must desire such a state wholeheartedly, seeking it as naturally and regularly as the air we breathe.

When we desire to grow spiritually, a good place to start is with our breathing, focusing on its rhythmic nature. All meditation and contemplation begins with breathing. Unlike New Year's resolutions and other such acts of resolve, which fade quickly, whenever you find yourself forgetting or losing your resolve to love and experience God, return to your breath. Find time to quiet yourself, using that moment as a reminder to re-center and refocus. This reminder should put a smile on your face and resolve in your heart, that this is who you wish to be and how you wish to live. All things are possible for those who believe, but they are less difficult for those who hope and easier for those who love. The burden is lightest for those who practice all three virtues, for as the apostle Paul declared, the entire substance of religion is faith, hope, and love (1 Cor. 13:13).

In our journey we must be careful not to proceed faster than grace allows. When progress seems slow, if at all, Brother Lawrence keeps it real, reminding us that "one does not become holy all at once." When we fail in our resolve, we can resume our practice with full confidence that God is merciful, always ready to receive us affectionately and without recrimination. This is the God of whom Paul wrote so poignantly: "For while we were still weak, at the right time Christ died for the ungodly . . . But God proves his love for us in that while we still were sinners, Christ died for us" (Rom. 5:6, 8). How can we neglect the presence of one who loves and affirms us unconditionally?

If the method I am describing sounds like the practice of mindfulness, the Buddhist-inspired approach to life that helps people dwell more fully and deeply in the present moment, there are similarities. Thich Nhat Hanh, the Vietnamese monk, taught Christians to use mindfulness as a way to enhance their awareness of God, as a means and not as an end.[2]

When Lawrence found himself wandering from his goal, he did not fret or become despondent. He merely found a way to refocus gently and quietly. He assured his readers that they should not become despondent when they lost focus, for their moods and timeframe could not control God. God is present, he believed, when we least expect it, nearer than we are aware. However, "to know God, we must think of Him often; and when we come to love Him, we shall then also think of Him often, for our heart will be with our treasure."[3]

When the demands of life distract me from my spiritual goal, I need reminders. I live on a high bluff overlooking the Ohio River, and trains run regularly along tracks on both sides of the river. A guest once counted over eighty trains a day passing far below—not one train with eighty cars, but eighty different trains, mostly carrying freight, many with over one hundred separate cars. When they pass, whether by day or night, they often blow a piercing whistle as they approach crossings along the way. I have learned to enjoy the sight and sounds of those trains, using their mournful whistles as reminders to refocus and resume concentration on God. If possible, I stop what I am doing and go to my meditation chair, where I practice structured relaxation. I take a couple of minutes to quiet my spirit

---

2. Hahn, *Living Buddha, Living Christ*, 15.
3. Lawrence, *Practice of the Presence*, 53.

before resuming my activities. Perhaps you too can find reminders when you fall short of your goal.

For the time being, consider setting aside whatever you are doing, including reading this chapter, in order to quiet your spirit and refocus spiritually. If you have practiced contemplation in the past, then do so now. Do not become concerned with the mechanics of contemplation; that will come later (see chapter 7). Simply find a quiet place, removed from any distractions, and initiate what will become for you a daily practice of sitting in silence (you can start with a span of two or three minutes, though eventually you will want to extend the time) to simply become aware of God's presence in your life.

Because our intent here is preparatory to the practice of contemplation, I provide only a few practical guidelines. Begin by sitting comfortably, with your eyes closed. Sit in a straight chair, with your back erect and both feet flat on the floor. To slouch indicates inattention and to cross the legs restricts the circulation. Rest your hands on your knees or thighs, palms up or down, whichever you find most comfortable.

Another way to focus is to concentrate on your breathing, buoyed by its calming and rhythmic nature. As you do, taking slow, deep breaths, you will find it reducing stress and any negative emotions lurking deep within. If thoughts intrude, focus on your breathing. As you practice regularly, the strength of habit will make it easier to let go of the normal flow of thoughts and distractions. At the end of the chosen time span, slowly return to your ordinary world and thoughts. This may be a good time to converse with God or to refocus your thoughts.

The spiritual journey has been likened to a growing tree. At first one sees only the trunk and the branches. Later come the leaves. These make the tree more attractive, and this stage of growth might be compared to the enjoyment that comes when you first enter interior silence. After the leaves come the flowers, another moment of intense satisfaction, but they soon die and fall to the ground. The fruit comes only at the end of the season, and even then, it takes a while to ripen on the tree. So one should not think when the leaves appear and the flowers bloom, that this is the end of the journey. The spiritual journey is long and is more like a wilderness trek than a quick climb up a hill. There will be defeats and disappointments, but each step forward is its own reward when in the company of Christ, "the pioneer and perfecter of our faith" (Heb. 12:2). So travel light, running with perseverance the race that is set before you, for the sake of the joy that awaits.

Like Brother Lawrence, who practiced the presence of God in the most ordinary activities of his day, I suggest the following daily activities as filled with promise. You may wish to add your own possibilities to the list.

- When you first arise, welcome the first person you meet, whether at home, work, or at play, as you would welcome God, with all care, attention, respect, and love.
- When you sit down to eat, chew each bite slowly and deliberately, as though you were eating the body of God. Food can be sacramental, and eating a way to commune with God and partake of God's essence. Likewise, when you drink coffee, tea, juice, or water, imagine you are drinking the living water of which Jesus spoke in John 4:14, a spring of water gushing forth into eternal life.
- If there are children in your home or in your life, treat each with the care and devotion you would give to the Christ child.
- If there are any pets in your house or neighborhood, or if you feed the birds, watch their behavior and, like Francis of Assisi, treat them as creatures beloved of God.
- As you drive to work or go shopping, drive as if God were a passenger in your car. What is God saying in each situation you observe or encounter? (If you are practicing the presence of God while driving, keep in mind that this practice is designed to give you greater awareness and make you a better driver, not make you more accident-prone.)
- When something undesirable or unwanted occurs during the day, imagine that it can only get to you after first coming through God. How should you respond? Can the misfortune or unwelcome experience contain something beneficial?
- When you go to bed at night, take a moment to reminisce and give thanks. How was God present in your life that day? What did God teach you? What did you learn?
- How did you glorify God today? Did you enjoy God's presence?

A Litmus Test: Generosity

A large percentage of people in their older years are frustrated, depressed, or angry. What an unfortunate way to live one's life. Those who encounter

God in their spiritual journey experience unexplainable transformation. They finally understand Paul's exuberance in 2 Corinthians 5:17–18: "So if anyone is in Christ, there is a new creation: everything old has passed away; see, everything has become new! All this is from God, who reconciled us to himself through Christ." The newness of which Paul speaks finally becomes their experience as well. Life becomes more spacious, the boundaries of their container having been enlarged. For many who encounter God, life is characterized by seven transformational qualities:[4]

1. Less fear and therefore less hostility.
2. Less combative.
3. Less need of attention.
4. Less assertive.
5. Less self-concerned.
6. Less dogmatic.
7. Less possessive.

As we close this chapter, I wish to focus on the last of these qualities. For most people, money is their chief possession, their final security. Money is a touchy subject, but it is one we need to address. Since we no longer live in a barter society, we need money in order to survive, not only enough to live on but also enough to carry us through the crises of life and our retirement years. But how much money is enough?

Like alcohol, drugs, gambling, and other vices, people can become addicted to money. This addiction can be dangerous because it can give people power over others and can drive them to take from the poor what little they have (addiction to power and wealth, by the way, are often intertwined). One of the strange characteristics of wealth addicts is that they seldom enjoy their money, as Philip Slater points out in his book *Wealth Addiction*. Whenever any one aspect of life becomes the total focus of our energy—our single goal—our lives go out of balance, and what we pursue can become evil. In fact, single-minded concentration on spiritual phenomena can be as corrupting as any addiction within the material world—whether it be to sex, approval, drugs, power, or wealth.

In the Bible, money is viewed in various ways, not always negatively. The Old Testament and the Jews of Jesus' time tended to see wealth as a

---

4. The following points are adapted from Rohr, *Falling Upward*, 118–125.

sign of God's favor. Because the Sadducees of biblical times did not believe in any real afterlife, they believed that rewards and punishments occurred in this life. Jesus, the Pharisees of his day, and all other Jews who believed in an afterlife, had a different understanding of life on earth. Because they viewed life on earth as not final, it was seen as a place to work on one's character and to care for those less fortunate, not a time to accumulate temporal wealth or material possessions. (The classic gospel passage on this topic is in the Sermon on the Mount; see Matt. 6:19–34.) As Jesus recognized, wealth can make people cruel and greedy. For this reason, Jesus told a wealthy youth who asked to become his follower to sell all he had and give it to the poor (Mark 10:17–27). While some Christians have taken this teaching as a prescription or requirement for all followers of Jesus, we must note that Jesus did not require poverty of everyone, any more than he demanded that all his followers be celibate.

Luke reports that some women supported Jesus' disciples from their property and accompanied the band of disciples in order to minister to them. On no occasion did Jesus suggest that they sell their possessions. Jesus' demands on the rich young man had to do with the particular person's circumstances. Jesus perceived great ability and sincerity in the one who had come and asked what he needed to do to be complete. However, Jesus also saw that the man was addicted to wealth and thus told him to sell everything he had, give it to the poor, and come and follow him. This was specific advice to a specific person, not a general rule for all.

Jesus never stated that the love of money was the root of all evil, a statement we read in 1 Timothy 6:10. He saw many sources of evil in the world, not simply one. Nevertheless, any aspect of our lives that keeps us from enjoying fellowship with the loving God and from sharing that love with others in concrete and practical ways can become evil. Certainly giving away all that one has opens a pathway for radical discipleship, but if it were not for those who have successful practices or profitable businesses, there would be no one to help those in need.

In the Bible, the concept of realizing and acting upon one's ordained position as God's co-worker (vice-regent) is called stewardship. The covenant of creation binds all humans to God and to one another. It entails that, as image-bearers, humans are to reflect God's concern for all of life. That includes using wealth and property for the benefit of the entire community. The Bible provides many examples of how this occurs, stressing the welfare of the poor (the fatherless, widow, and sojourner; the book of

James in the New Testament powerfully summarizes this concept in 1:27: "Religion that is pure and undefiled before God, the Father, is this: to care for orphans and widows in their distress . . ."). In Deuteronomy 24:19–22 God instructs the Israelites to harvest their fields only once a season; what remains is reserved for the needy. Leviticus 23:22 commands farmers not to harvest their land to the borders, but to leave the produce at the edges for the poor. The Bible also contains strict regulations regarding lending practices (Exod. 22:25–27), provides for an impartial judicial process (Deut. 16:18–20), and for paying the poor and needy worker on the day they earn their hire (Deut. 24:14–15). Partiality and bribery are denounced, and the Hebrews are warned to protect strangers and foreigners in their midst, for God protected them while they were strangers in Egypt (Exod. 22:21–24). As Deuteronomy 16:20 makes clear, the concept of stewardship embodies the principle of justice, and, indirectly, of righteousness and steadfast love: "Justice, and only justice, you shall pursue, so that you may live and occupy the land that the Lord your God is giving you."

From the Bible, churches have promoted the principle of the tithe (see Lev. 23:30–32; 2 Chr. 31:5–6; Mal. 3:8–10), a form of stewardship based on the giving of one tenth of our earnings to religious institutions and to those less fortunate than ourselves. While financial giving is a legitimate form of stewardship, we need to heed Paul's reminder that we can give all we have, but if we are not motivated by love—if we are not demonstrating genuine love, compassion, and forgiveness to others—then our actions are without value (1 Cor. 13:3).

It is nearly impossible to remain in contact with the realm of the Spirit unless we give not only our material substance but also our time and talents for religious and charitable purposes. For how can we justify our connection with Christ and with the power and love of God's kingdom if we spend all but a tiny fraction of our resources on ourselves, on our desires and interests, or on the quest for more money? To say that we are sincere and truly committed and to remain in such a selfish frame of mind is hypocritical. It is clearly not what discipleship is about. For those who do not give of their substance, the spiritual realm usually closes and remains closed.

Unless we give of our resources to institutions that—however imperfect, inadequate, and fragile—are dedicated to the realm of the Spirit and to outreach to those who need love, medical care, housing, and food, the religious impulse and encounter usually falters. Of course, in this age of social predation and electronic guile, we need to know that our giving is not just feathering someone's nest or aiding someone's ambitions.

In our giving, we need not be bound by some formula, as if giving one tenth of one's financial resources satisfies some commandment or duty. Such an understanding of the tithe is self-defeating, for this rationale gives people the idea that their obligation to God and to others can be dismissed with a tip. Authentic commitment to God and to others requires us to give of our time and energy as well as our money, possibly adding up to more than a tip.

Those who find their giving transformed are in for a great surprise, for those who give away a sizeable portion of their resources find their priorities changing: they find themselves spending more time reading the Bible and other worthwhile literature, as well as more time meditating, praying, listening, and caring for those in need. In the process they discover a sacramental way of living, a reminder that practicing the presence of God results in practical forms of commitment to God and to others. Those who give to God and for God discover the presence of God's kingdom to be an ever-present reality.

As we examine the biblical teaching on generosity, we need to take inventory. How well are we doing in the area of stewardship? If Christians fail to lead the way in justice, righteousness, compassion, and stewardship, does God have a back-up plan?

Questions for Discussion and Reflection

1. Is there a person, place, or thing that best represents a "thin place" in your life? Explain your answer.

2. What are the basic differences between the kataphatic and apophatic approaches to God? Which do you prefer? Why? Does your church or worshipping community provide you adequate support in your spiritual journey? Why or why not?

3. Brother Lawrence indicated that he often felt closer to God in mundane activities than while performing strictly devotional or religious duties. Has this been your experience as well? Explain your answer.

4. Is it possible to be hyperspiritual, that is, overly zealous, in the Christian life? If so, can you provide examples?

5. What does the phrase "purity of heart" mean to you (see Matthew 5:8)?

6. Have there been times in your life when your experience of God was a joy or delight? If so, describe your experience.

7. Christianity teaches that God is love, and that God loves us unconditionally. Often we focus so much on our need to love God that we miss the experience of being loved by God. Have you ever experienced God's love? Can you describe how you felt?

8. When you feel you have lost your way or compromised your priorities spiritually, how do you get back on track? Are there reminders in your life to keep you focused? Is so, what are they? If not, why not?

9. Read over the bulleted list of recommended activities near the end of the chapter. Can you think of other activities you would like to add to the list?

10. What, for you, seems easiest and most natural about practicing the presence of God? What seems most difficult or unnatural about this method?

11. *For personal reflection*: Is there an area of your life that needs transformation? Where must God begin in stripping you of your old self?

12. *For personal reflection*: What role does money play in your life? If you were to ask God to make you more generous, where should God begin?

CHAPTER 6

Experiencing God through Jesus Christ

God was in Christ, reconciling the world to himself.

—2 Corinthians 5:19

Within each of us is a deep desire for intimacy with God, with our truest self, and with all of creation. Because life is difficult, and we are wired for survival, we develop coping mechanisms that separate us from each other and from God. Thankfully, God is patient and has many ways to reach us.

Jesus is one of the clearest images of God's love. His teaching and example model for us what it means to be both human and divine—at the same time. He dismantles our preconceived ideas about who and where God is and is not. Jesus made room for the new by letting go of the old. John the Baptist described Jesus as a "winnowing fork" that separates the grain from the chaff (see Matt. 3:12). If we don't winnow, we spend a lot of time protecting the "chaff" or non-essentials. Jesus did not let the old get in the way of the new, but rather revealed what the old was saying all along. Jesus conserved what was worth conserving and prevented non-essentials from getting in the way. While honoring and emphasizing the core elements of his tradition, he ignored and even undercut most non-essential religious rules and norms. This is invariably the character of any reformer, to follow the Spirit's leading.

When I ask the question, "Who came first, Jesus or Christ?" people respond with bewilderment, for the question seems ignorant or baffling, presenting a conundrum similar to that of the chicken and the egg. When we speak of Jesus, aren't we speaking of "Christ," and isn't Christ a reference to Jesus? Speaking theologically, and in hindsight, they may well be the same. However, for the sake of our discussion, I wish to maintain the historical distinction.

The expression "Jesus Christ," used in this chapter's heading, is not intended as a name but as a title. During the lifetime of the historical person we think of as Jesus, his contemporaries would have called him "Jesus," a common name at that time. To distinguish him from others, they might have used the more specific reference "Jesus of Nazareth." The term "Christ" (*Christos* in Greek) was added later, and only by his followers. At first *Christos* (meaning "The Anointed One") was used of Jesus because he was believed to be the long-awaited Messiah, a term that in Hebrew also means "one anointed or appointed to a sacred office." In time, the term came to mean much more, including a preexistent deity, the incarnate deity, and the second member of the Trinity.

Although it is not my intention to debate the joining of "Jesus" and "Christ" doctrinally—Christians do view Jesus to be the Christ and vice versa—for the time being I wish to preserve their distinction. When we focus on experiencing God through Jesus, we emphasize the humanity of Jesus and rely on the Synoptic Gospels, thinking of what Jesus taught during his lifetime about God. When we focus on experiencing God through Christ, we emphasize the eternal member of the Trinity, the preexistent and divine being who became incarnate in Jesus, who acted and spoke through Jesus both before and after the resurrection as the Cosmic Christ. For this understanding we rely on the Gospel of John as well as later Christian teaching about Christ. The fundamental affirmation of Christianity is that Jesus is the clue to *Christos*, just as Christ is the clue to the mystery of God and to the meaning of human existence.

Experiencing God through Jesus

When we think of Jesus, I suggest we think of the historical human being who represents for Christians the ideal universal person, the embodiment of the highest and best in us all. At this initial point in our discussion, then, we will focus on the Jesus of history, the one who bears the ideal of normality and universality simultaneously.

Had Jesus no other legacy, he would be remembered as one of the world's master teachers. Jesus, however, did not come on the scene to conform to anyone's preconceived expectation about sages, or for that matter, about prophets or messiahs. His subject, essentially, was threefold: he made known something about God, something about humankind, and something about their interrelationship.

Apart from the tradition of Judaism, however, the life or teaching of Jesus would have been incomprehensible. In Jesus' day there was a vast human quest for God, wrapped up in piety and legalism (Judaism), and in idolatry and superstition (Gentiles). The Jews were monotheists and had a central temple in Jerusalem, dedicated to sacrifice and rituals. Much of their worship was motivated by duty and regulated by tradition. However, no code of laws can deal with the variety of human beings. While Jesus affirmed the value of Jewish law in many of his actions and teachings, he regularly pointed beyond the law. According to Jesus, each of us has individual value and our own unique journey to God.

When the institutional element dominates religion, there is often an obsession with the organization and with the details of its regulations. Blind obedience is required. This often results in institutional rigidity and sterility. When religion becomes only a matter of outer rules and rituals, then those who deviate from the accepted practices and beliefs are not tolerated. Such religious prejudice drives thoughtful people away from the institutional church. The implications of Christian teaching can be ignored when we only accept tradition by rote. It took eighteen hundred years before Jesus' teaching of the equal value of all human beings resulted in the abolition of slavery. It took even longer before women were accorded the place that Jesus gave them. Cultural accretions quite at variance to a religion often creep into religious tradition to corrupt and dilute it. For that reason tradition needs continued reaffirming experiences of God, reflection, a knowledge of what makes us human, and love. Without them religion can become destructive and oppressive.

In his book *Jesus of Nazareth*, the German scholar Günther Bornkamm pointed out that Jesus added only two basic new elements to Judaism: his teaching about God and about God's kingdom or rule on earth. In this segment our focus will be on these elements, and on Jesus' unique points of emphasis.

Today, when we think of the kingdom or rule of God, it is easy to miss the original meaning of the concept. We relate the concept of rule to that of servitude, which sounds far too authoritarian. We think of theocracy as a form of government that suppresses human freedom, but for the Jews of Jesus' time, the kingdom of God represented hope for the establishment of a just and ideal form of government. The coming of the kingdom of God was expected to end unjust rule. Its coming would establish peace between nations, between individuals, and within all human beings. This is the "abundance of life" of which Jesus speaks in John 10:10. Jesus' message of the coming of God's kingdom, then, should be seen in the context of humanity's search for peace, freedom, justice, and life.

The Old Testament traces the emergence of monotheism in history. Gradually the Hebrew people moved from seeing Yahweh as the god of the nation (henotheism) to perceiving the Lord as the one and only God. The Israelites were also much interested in this world and in cultivating the goodness of life on earth. However, they were not materialists, for they lived in a world where the physical and spiritual realms were equally real and important. Dreams and visions were viewed as messengers from the spiritual realm, and prophets were gifted with knowledge and wisdom that did not come through the five senses.

When we come to the New Testament, we find an even clearer emphasis on the reality of the spiritual world. God's kingdom was at hand, and the rule of evil was being defeated. The first major departure of Jesus from the Jewish tradition was his declaration that God's kingdom was present within human beings: "the kingdom of God is within (*entos*) you" (Luke 17:21, KJV, NIV). We do not know the Aramaic rendering of the Greek word *entos*, but as John Sanford pointed out in his book *The Kingdom Within*, at least twelve early church fathers translated the Greek as "within" you and never as "among" you (NRSV) or "in the midst" of you (RSV). There is a world of difference between God's kingdom being present among people and within them, in the sense of being accessible now, in the depth of their being.

In the tradition of the Old Testament and of Judaism, the coming of the kingdom of God meant the coming of God, and not merely the emergence of some surrogate situation or institution. The center of eschatological hope was the "Day of Yahweh," the time or times appointed by God for justice, vindication, and judgment. When Jesus proclaims that "the kingdom of God has come near" or "is at hand" (Mark 1:15), he is saying that "God is near or at hand." The kingdom of God, in other words, does not primarily imply a realm, but God's presence as Lord. The message of Jesus appears to be that God's reign, that is, that God's direct presence, is now available. In Jesus and through his ongoing work in us, God's eternal reality (heaven) has come close to earth. We find this understanding in the second petition of the Lord's Prayer: "Your kingdom come, your will be done, on earth as it is in heaven" (Matt. 6:10). As Jesus teaches in this model prayer, God is not distant, in a far-off heaven, unconcerned with human affairs. God is among us, around us, even within us. Human encounter with God is not relegated to the distant future or far removed from us in space. It is near at hand. It can be experienced now, in the dimension of our humanity. By emphasizing God's nearness in the present, however, we are not negating the biblical expectation of the consummation of God's purpose and will in some future sense, for God's kingdom will not be completely established until all evil and rebellion are overcome.

While many Christians today focus on the second coming of Christ, it is important to recognize that in the early Christian message the focus lay not in the anticipation of Christ's return but in the proclamation that Christ's "first coming" was itself an eschatological event, decisive and final. The New Testament places the emphasis on the victory that has already been won in the cross and resurrection and shuns any attempt to pry into the mystery of the future, which lies in the sole authority of God (Acts 1:7; Matt. 24:26). Oscar Cullmann expressed this matter aptly using an analogy from World War II. Speaking of the invasion at Normandy, known as the Decisive Day (D-day), he noted that the decisive battle in a war may occur at a relatively early stage of the war, and yet the war continues. While World War II continued until Victory Day (V-day), the tide turned on D-day, guaranteeing the final outcome.[1] As a result of Christ's resurrection, early Christians were assured that the goal of history had been achieved proleptically by Christ's victory over death. The End would merely vindicate the faith of the present.

Even though we human beings cannot hasten God's kingdom or presence by our actions, whether conservative or progressive, evolutionary or revolutionary, passivity is not efficacious. In Jesus' parables, the insistent widow continues to call out, and the neighbor knocks at his friend's door at night for a long time before he is answered. People who do nothing usually get nowhere.

Another unique message of Jesus was his teaching concerning God. Jesus spoke of God as Father, as one who could only be approached through spiritual worship (John 4:23–24). When Jesus revealed God's character as Love (John 3:16), all existing worship, whether pagan or monotheistic, came under question as misguided or inadequate. Under Jesus' guidance, for the first time worshippers could address the Creator of the world as *abba* (Mark 14:36; see Rom. 8:15; Gal. 4:6), meaning "daddy." This is how Jesus chose to address God in prayer. Such an expression would have appeared to many Jews as unceremonious and lacking in respect. *Abba*, an Aramaic

---

1. Cullmann, *Christ and Time*, 84.

term, goes back to the earliest biblical records about Jesus. It is a child's familiar address to a father on earth, completely uncommon in religious language of Jesus' time. More than "Father," the word contains something of the quality we associate with mothering. A greater understanding of God, a more transformative perspective, has never been imparted.

Through instruction on prayer, in parable, and by teaching, Jesus indicated that God, the creative power at the center of the cosmos, is loving and caring as a devoted parent. This love is not one aspect of God, but is the organizing reality at the heart of things. The revelation that God is love does not imply that we do not have to do anything to receive it. Because love is a gift, it cannot be earned or be forced upon anyone; but it must be received. Our attitude toward God, our response to God's love, determines how much love we receive.

While Jesus changed the way we understand God, the God of the Old Testament had been speaking to humanity through an entire history of dialogue with Israel. As Walter Brueggemann indicates in his *Theology of the Old Testament*, the God that Jesus incarnated was already seen to be "merciful, gracious, faithful, forgiving, and steadfast in love" (Exod. 34:6–7). This "credo of adjectives," positive and relational in nature, announce the character of God, indicating God's intense solidarity, loyalty, and commitment to those with whom he is related.[2]

Much as we need to unlearn harsh and damning views of God, we also must unlearn many of the ways we have been taught about dealing with other human beings. There seems to be only one demand that this God of love lays upon those who receive love and forgiveness, namely, to treat those around them as they have been treated by God. That is the litmus test of all spiritual transformation.

Experiencing God through Christ

The story of Jesus does not end with his death. It begins anew with his resurrection. As a result, the dispersed band of Jesus' disciples gathered anew, and through their belief in Jesus and their hope for his return as Lord and King, became a community. Their witness awakened new faith, giving birth to the church and supporting its mission to expand throughout the earth. As the New Testament indicates, the preacher from Galilee entered the message of faith as its content; he who called others to believe became the object of that

---

2. Brueggemann, *Theology of the Old Testament*, 215–28.

faith. As the followers of Jesus attest, "We have come to believe and know that you are the Holy One of God" (John 6:69).

Understanding the process by which Jesus became known as "Christ," the incarnate deity, is not easy, for it involves expertise in theology and philosophy and familiarity with three ancient mindsets: Jewish, Hellenistic, and Christian. While readers need not follow every step of the argument presented in this chapter, the explanation is designed to clarify what Christians mean by the "Cosmic Christ," and how this theme enhances our worship and relationship with God.

Early Christians set forth their confession in many different forms, through sermons, in hymns and prayers, and in creedal statements. These expressions, repeated in various forms at baptism and the Lord's Supper, in preaching and teaching, in the struggle against false teaching, and in the witness of the martyrs, all address Jesus of Nazareth by the compound name "Jesus Christ" or simply by the titles "Christ" or "Lord." There are many titles for Jesus in the New Testament, but none more significant that these, for they signify about Jesus a transition from mortal humanity to eternal divinity, from God's representative on earth to a heavenly being come to earth "for us and our salvation," as the Nicene Creed declares. Such language, of which the New Testament and the Christian tradition are full, represents an entire range of statements about Jesus as the Christ. These cluster around the concept of preexistence—of an eternal, heavenly being who enters history to dwell with humanity. "God was in Christ," Paul tells believers in 2 Corinthians 5:19, "reconciling the world to himself." According to this perspective, if humans wish to experience God and understand God's ways with them, they must understand Christ and his ways.

An understanding of Christ currently in vogue, particularly among progressive Catholic thinkers such as Matthew Fox and Richard Rohr, is the concept of the Cosmic Christ, or what Rohr calls "the Universal Christ." Like Fox's earlier book, *Original Blessing* (1983), which introduced a shift in religious thinking from "original sin" to "original blessing," his later book, *The Coming of the Cosmic Christ* (1988), explored another paradigm shift, moving from concern with the historical Jesus to concern with the Cosmic Christ. According to Fox, this shift in understanding affects every aspect of culture, including how we relate to God, one another, and our planet.

The theme of the Cosmic Christ was vital to New Testament Christians, the Greek theologians of the patristic period, and was richly developed in the West by medieval creation-centered mystics such as Hildegard of Bingen, Francis of Assisi, Meister Eckhart, and Julian of Norwich, theologians such as Thomas Aquinas, and writers such as Dante Alighieri. However, this living cosmology was lost during the Enlightenment, when rationalism and patriarchal mindsets drove out mysticism, intuition, and religious imagination. If Newton was correct, and our universe is essentially a machine, who needs a Cosmic Christ?

For Rohr, the term "Christ" represents the eternal union of matter and Spirit from the beginning of time.[3] In Jesus, God's formlessness took on form in someone we could "hear, see, and touch" (1 John 1:1), making God easier to love. The expression "Cosmic Christ" views Christ cosmically, not as a solitary figure but as a universal reality that includes all humanity and all of creation since the beginning of time (see Romans 1:20): whenever the material and the spiritual coincide, there is the Christ. According to this perspective, Christ (and therefore God) need not be viewed as "out there" or "over there," for God is in us, here, now, and everywhere. Each human is a little word of God, a mini-incarnation of divine love. The goal, however, is not to focus on ourselves but to move beyond ourselves, recognizing that what's true in us is true in others as well. The Universal Christ permeates all creation; human beings are the image and likeness of God!

If we consciously take this Christ Mystery as our worldview, it creates immense joy and peace, for human beings are no longer alienated from God, others, or the universe. All people belong, indeed all things belong. Conversely, this view also requires embracing the sufferings of our lives; it means entering into darkness, the unknown corners of our lives, and learning to trust the darkness. It also means willing to sacrifice all we have for all that we can become in the power of God's love.

A Christian, according to this paradigm, is one who has learned to see Christ everywhere. For Rohr, wherever the human and the divine coexist, whenever the spiritual and the material coincide, in that moment, event, or person, we witness "the Second Coming of Christ." The Eucharist offers Christians the message in condensed form. "Eat it and know who you are," Augustine said. The expression "We are what we drink and eat" holds true spiritually as well as physically. The Cosmic Christ mindset encourages us to see Christ everywhere, in nature, in other religions, in other people, and

---

3. The Rohr material is taken from his daily online meditations, "The Universal Christ," December 2–7, 2018. Additional information may be found in Rohr's CD, "The Cosmic Christ," Center for Action and Contemplation, 2009, and in his newest publication, *The Universal Christ*, 2019.

within ourselves. In this sense, "Christ" is not only a name we give to Jesus, it is our Christian theological name as well.

How did this idea arise, this sense of a Cosmic Christ? The roots are said to lie in ancient Jewish wisdom literature as well as in Hellenistic philosophy. Because of its deeply symbolic character, the Cosmic Christ influenced christological hymns embedded in the New Testament, particularly those that utilize wisdom motifs to express Christian belief in the incarnation of Jesus (John 1:1-18) and in his cosmic rule (Col. 1:15-20). Among the various influences on the New Testament was the identification of Wisdom (Christ) with divine Spirit (2 Cor. 3:16-18), Word (John 1:1), and Law (Matt. 5:17-20; 7:24-29). Like Wisdom in the book of Proverbs and in the Intertestamental books of Sirach (Ecclesiasticus) and the Wisdom of Solomon, Christ preexisted his historical incarnation (Prov. 8:22-31). Having lived in intimate relation with God, Christ is now exalted and enthroned in heaven (Phil. 2:6-11).

Once Wisdom became identified with Jesus of Nazareth, and Jesus became an object of worship for early Jewish Christians, some of these same people, steeped in Jewish wisdom traditions, appropriated the hymn-like praise of personified Wisdom in order to express their devotion to Jesus Christ. The christological hymn fragments found in the Pauline corpus (Phil. 2:6-11; Col. 1:15-20; 1 Tim. 3:16), the Gospel of John (1:1-5, 9-14), and Hebrews (1:2-4) are fundamentally expressions of a Wisdom Christology that goes back to early Jewish Christianity.

The earliest use of christological hymn fragments is found in the Pauline corpus, and Paul likely heard such hymns in contexts where Greek was the primary language of worship, since hymns such as the one in Philippians 2 and particularly in Colossians 1 so clearly draw on the Greek text of the Wisdom of Solomon and were surely first composed in Greek. To judge from the fact that one finds hymn fragments in places as varied as Hebrews, the Fourth Gospel, and the Pauline corpus, such hymns and their composition must have been widespread. These hymns suggest a widely held common form of Wisdom Christology in early Christianity.

Wisdom thinking, to the extent that it is theology, is essentially a form of creation theology, and one should not be surprised to find in Christian wisdom hymns a considerable emphasis on what was true of the Son before and during the event of creation, including the doctrine of his preexistence and in due course a doctrine of the incarnation. In these hymns, Christ's career is envisioned as having both heavenly and earthly scope, and the attempt to express adequately the theological significance of this career led early Jewish Christians to draw on the most exalted language they could find—Jewish wisdom speculation, coupled with messianic interpretation of the Psalms and soteriological reflections on Christ's death.

Adolf von Harnack (1851–1930), the eminent German church historian, once wrote that the most important step ever taken in the domain of Christian doctrine was when the author of John's Gospel near the end of the first century equated Jesus with the Logos (see John 1:1–18). This passage has impacted belief in the divinity and preexistence of Christ more than any other New Testament passage. Here the early church derived its Logos Christology (i.e. the Son of God as the "Word") and its basic understanding of the incarnation.

There is in this hymn an obvious dependence on Genesis 1. Both documents begin with the words, "In the beginning," and in both God is said to create by means of the spoken word. The use of the Genesis material in the hymnic material about Wisdom both in the Hebrew Bible (see Prov. 3; 8:1—9:6) and in the later Jewish wisdom tradition inspires the ideas in this hymn. In that tradition one learns that personified Wisdom was present at creation, and that she calls God's people back to ethical living and offers them life and divine favor. These are the same things said of the Word in John's prologue. By 180 BCE, when Ben Sira wrote Sirach, this sort of Wisdom speculation included Torah, seen as the consummate expression of Wisdom (cf. Sir. 24). At the end of the Logos Hymn it is said that the Son eclipses this Torah, for through Torah came the law, but through the Logos come grace and truth (John 1:17).

One need not reiterate all the parallels between this hymn and the Jewish wisdom literature, although central to that correspondence is that Wisdom provides life and light (see John 1:4 and Wisdom 7:26, where Wisdom is said to be the reflection of eternal light, and Wisdom 7:25a, where she is the very life breath of God). The Wisdom of Solomon personifies *logos* in 18:15, when it declares that God's "all-powerful word leaped from heaven, from the royal throne" (18:15). Since Wisdom 9:10 had already said that Wisdom was present and sent forth from the throne, one can see how interchangeable the terms "wisdom" and "word" are in Wisdom of Solomon. This is also the case in Sirach 24:3, where Wisdom is said to come forth from the mouth of God. Another idea unique to John's prologue, the tabernacling of the Logos with God's people (John 1:14), is also manifest in

Sirach 24:8, where the Creator chooses a place for Wisdom to tent, namely in the earthly tabernacle in Zion (Sir. 24:10).

When the early Jewish Christians composed christological hymns, they searched for exalted language from their heritage that gave adequate expression to their newfound faith in Jesus Christ. No language seemed better suited for their task than the poems about personified or hypostasized Wisdom found in Proverbs 8, Job 28, Sirach 24, and Wisdom 7 and 9. In particular, it was the latest of these sapiential writings, the Wisdom of Solomon, that had the greatest impact. When the sapiential liturgical material was applied to the historical Jesus, the result is a very high Christology, predicating preexistence, incarnation, and even divinity to a historical person. The existence of these hymns in so many different sorts of sources—Pauline, Johannine, and in Hebrews—strongly suggests that Wisdom Christology was both widespread and popular with a variety of Christian writers and their audiences.

Since Logos as a concept was widespread before Christianity and contemporaneous with its start, we need to consider its place in Judaism and among Greek philosophers. Ancient Greek philosophers known as the Stoics held the concept of Logos in high esteem. For them it meant "word," as in the act of speaking, but it carried much deeper meaning. The word Logos, from which we get the English term "logic," also means "reason," and the Stoics believed that Logos (reason) was a divine element that infused all reality. There is, they believed, a rationality to the way things work, and if one wants to understand the world and how best to live, then one must seek to understand this underlying logic. Such understanding is both possible and practical because Logos was believed to reside in every human being. Each person, it turns out, has a portion of Logos within, and if we apply our minds to the world, we can understand it. And if we understand this underlying logic, we can live peaceful, enriched lives.

Thinkers who stood directly in the line of the great philosopher Plato took the idea of the Logos in a different direction. For them the Logos functions as a mediator or bridge between the two essential constituents of reality, connecting spirit and matter. For Platonists, the eternal Logos is what allows spirit to interact with matter, the nondivine with the divine. Though humans are thoroughly immersed in the material world, the presence of the Logos within our material bodies allows us to escape our material entrapment and attain spiritual wisdom and enlightenment (see John 1:9).

Familiarity with some of these ideas enabled Jewish thinkers to connect these Stoic and Platonic ideas with their own. In the Hebrew Bible, for example, God creates all things by speaking a "word": "And God said, 'Let there be light'; and there was light" (Gen. 1:3). Jewish thinkers, influenced by Greek thought, naturally associated the "Word of God" with the Logos. For them the Logos comes from God, and since it is God's Logos, in a sense it is God. However, once this Word is stated, it comes be to be understood as a distinct entity, separate from God. Thus the Logos came to be seen in some Jewish circles as a hypostasis (such a possibility is implied already in the Hebrew Bible; see, for example, 1 Samuel 3:1, 7). The outworking of this conception is evident in the most famous Jewish philosopher of antiquity, Philo of Alexandria (20 BCE–CE 50), a contemporary of Jesus.

Philo maintained that the Logos was the highest of all beings, the image of God according to which and by which the universe is ordered. God's Logos was, in particular, the model according to which humans were created. It is easy to see that Philo is taking functions assigned to Wisdom, such as creating and ordering all things, and attributing them to the Logos. The two are so closely associated by Philo that there is a sense in which Wisdom gives birth to Logos. Philo uses a wide array of terms to describe Logos, including: "firstborn son," "archangel," "Name of God," and "governor and administrator of all things." Because the Logos is God's Logos, it is divine and can be called by divine names. Philo also describes the full complement of divine attributes, which include "the creative power," "the royal power," "the gracious power," and the legislative powers by which God prescribes and prohibits acts, and over all these he places the "divine Logos" as chief of God's powers. Because the Logos is God, and God is God, Philo sometimes speaks of "two gods," and elsewhere of Logos as "the second God." But there is a difference for Philo between "the God" and "a god," and Logos is the latter.

The christological use of Logos in the Johannine writings is based upon the conviction of Jesus' cosmic lordship adapted to the appreciation of a particular audience, for whom the expression was especially meaningful. Both in New Testament times and later, the Johannine Logos offered rich christological possibilities. In addition, the concept offered an effective bridge to contemporary culture, opening the way for Christians to dialogue meaningfully with non-Christian thinkers. By maintaining that the entire world was created by Logos, early Christians universalized their understanding of Jesus as divine agent of all creation and therefore as cosmic Lord.

While the topic of Christology is central to John, the Gospel does not approach the topic abstractly or metaphysically but relationally, in association with the notion of discipleship, with what it means to be a believer (see John 1:12, 14, 16, 18). While religious traditions rooted in a historical figure traditionally develop claims for the uniqueness of the founder as well as his or her revelation, for John it is not Jesus' experience that is central but rather it is the believers' experience of Jesus.

The presence of Logos Christology, inserted in the prologue but obviously central to the Fourth Gospel, takes a concept current in Hellenistic philosophies but also central to Jewish thought and plies its imaginative richness to suggest that in one person Jesus fulfills simultaneously the variety of religious and philosophical views of the universe. For John, Jesus Christ is Stoic Logos, Hebraic Word of God, and Jewish Wisdom all in one. Nevertheless, the thrust of the prologue seems to be that for the Christian, Logos is a person and not an abstract philosophical concept.

The Beyond in the Midst

As we have discovered, Christology is not simply about Jesus and who he was. It is also about anthropology—about what it means to be human—and it is necessarily about God, the ineffable mystery of reality. Contemporary theologians are in agreement that a dualistic model of the universe is no longer viable. Whether examined from the outside or the inside, reality is now viewed as a whole. The traditional divisions with which theology has worked—body and soul, earth and heaven, this world and the next, the secular and the sacred, the natural and the supernatural, the two natures human and divine, I and Thou—are decreasingly useful. In our pluralistic world, however, this need not mean a repudiation of uniqueness or individualism.

For theology, the implication is not the reduction of the transcendent to pure naturalism. Rather it is an apprehension of the "beyond in the midst," of the transcendent in, with, and under the imminent. It is the refusal to see any final discontinuity between the human spirit and the Spirit of God.

The best theological model—perhaps the only appropriate model today—for a satisfactory conception of God and of the incarnation, is named "panentheism." This perspective finds the Being of God including and penetrating the entire universe, but (as against pantheism) God's Being is more than the universe. According to this view, God is in everything and everything is in God. Yet God is greater still. Unlike pantheism, which depersonalizes and dehistoricizes, panentheism personalizes reality, seeking God as the inner truth, depth, and center of all being.

When speaking of God, words are bound to fail. Paucity of words has always been a mark of the mystics, as acknowledged by the ancient Daoist poet Lao Tzu: "He who knows does not speak. He who speaks does not know."[4] One of the insights of our time is that the transpersonal character of God is better expressed not by envisaging God as a bigger and better Individual or as a collective Personality incorporating all other persons, but in terms of the interpersonal. In this sense the Jewish philosopher Martin Buber taught that in the beginning—and in the end—is not the individual, the "I" or even the "Thou," but the joint "I-Thou." This image of God goes beyond pantheism, deism, and traditional theism, in that it views the whole of reality ultimately not in terms of a monarchical Being supreme among individual entities, but of a divine "field" in which finite Thous are constituted in the freedom of personalizing love. This is the vision to which the New Testament points, of God as "all in all" (1 Cor.15:28; cf. Rom. 11:36; Eph. 1:23).

Ultimately, of course, there are things we cannot think up or express, but when we hear them or see them we say, "Yes." There is the sense that what is most real is before us; we are simply catching up to it, entering into it. Pascal's remark is haunting: "You would not be seeking me if you had not found me." Life is response—and hence responsibility—to "the beyond in the midst." The Christian gospel is that human beings are responsible—terrifyingly so—in freedom to a God whose strength is made perfect in weakness (2 Cor. 12:9). One of the distinctive features of this gospel is the utterly intimate relationship that it sums up in Jesus' word for God: *abba* (father or daddy). We too can use this word with regard to God (Rom. 8:15–17). It is this relationship at the heart of the universe, at the core of reality, that biblical Christology addresses.

An important point to remember is that no title or name for Jesus, from all that have come down to us from Judaism or been taken over from the religious language of Hellenism, retains its meaning unchanged. Likewise, christological titles take on the mystery of Jesus Christ and acquire new meanings, reflecting their symbolic and expansive nature.

---

4. *Tao Te Ching*, 56.

I have spoken elsewhere of the "translation principle" in Christianity, and of Christ as "the Eternal Word of God Translated."[5] This idea, taken from missiologist Andrew Walls, views the incarnation not as a static concept, its meaning immutable and fixed for all time, but as an act of translation. When God in Christ became man, divinity was translated into humanity, as though humanity were a receptor language. Translation, however, is not a precise art but a high risk business. Exact transmission of meaning from one linguistic medium to another is continually hampered by structural and cultural differences. The words of the receptor language are pre-loaded, and meanings in the source language commingle with those of the receptor to create uncharted possibilities.

The Christian faith, reflecting its missionary inclination and its incarnational calling, is repeatedly coming into creative interaction with new cultures, traditions, and different systems of thought. That means that Christianity's profoundest expressions are often local, vernacular, and temporal.

Questions for Discussion and Reflection

1. From your perspective, which seems more natural, to consider experiencing God or Jesus Christ? Explain your answer.

2. In your estimation, who came first, Jesus or Christ? Explain your answer.

3. In your estimation, how is *Jesus* the clue to the mystery of God and to the meaning of human existence?

4. In your estimation, how is *Christ* the clue to the mystery of God and to the meaning of human existence?

5. Do you agree with Bornkamm that Jesus added only two basic new elements to Judaism? Can you think of any besides Jesus' teaching about God and about God's kingdom on earth?

6. After reading this chapter, what did you learn about the concept of God's kingdom?

7. What does Cullmann's analogy from World War II teach (or clarify) about the kingdom of God?

---

5. Vande Kappelle, *Iron Sharpens Iron*, 3–5; *Refined by Fire*, 5–7.

8. After reading this chapter, what did you learn concerning God and God's character that can change how you worship and relate to God?

9. How does the concept of the Cosmic Christ represent a paradigm shift for Christians?

10. How does the concept of the Cosmic Christ change how you relate to God, others, and to nature?

11. What is Logos Christology, and how does it help us relate to Jesus and to God?

CHAPTER 7

Experiencing God through Prayer, Meditation, and Silence

God comes disguised as your life.

—Paula D'Arcy

During my formative years, when I was formulating my Christian worldview, I learned that religion was essentially a one-way street: God took the initiative (that was called "revelation," which was found primarily in the Bible), and humans responded (that was called "worship"), individually (through prayer and Bible reading) and corporately (in church). Another form of response was through witness (called "evangelism") and service. Service meant performing deeds of kindness and compassion, as well as contributing financially to the church (called "tithes") and to other worthwhile causes (called "offerings").

While God's primary revelation occurred long ago, during biblical times, God could still speak to individuals today, through the Holy Spirit. Believers were encouraged to have daily devotions—that is, a time of Bible reading and prayer—because it was through such activities, in addition to church worship, that God might speak directly to us. During these times we might expect guidance for daily living and gain a clearer understanding of biblical teaching, but only as clarification of what had previously been recorded in scripture, for individual insight could never contradict inspired truth.

As I progressed in my faith, I often questioned why divine revelation was relegated to one specific historical period, and that several thousand years in the past, and why such revelation was limited initially to one geographical region (Israel) and to one ethnic group (Jews). Why didn't God speak decisively today, I wondered? Was God unable to do so, or were modern humans somehow less able to receive revelation than their ancient counterparts?

Eventually I came to realize that my thinking was wrong, that it was driven by faulty questioning. God had never stopped communicating with humanity, and modern human beings are still able to receive revelation from God. Eventually I came to realize what Friedrich von Hügel had emphasized persuasively in his writings, that holistic religion is comprised of three elements in creative tension with each other. First, mature religion has a historical or institutional element, resulting in a religious tradition that has been refined through practice.[1] Secondly, it required a mystical or emotional element, a direct experience of God. Thirdly, mature religion requires an intellectual or scientific element, including the refinement developed by rationality and the capacity for critical, analytical thought.

If religious practice neglects intellectual and scientific scrutiny, it can become weighed down with superstitious accretions, outdated cultural patterns, and self-serving ethical practices. Powerless to engage fully with the values and mindset of the generation in which it lives, such religion will lack the ability to express to others its truth in viable terms.

However, if religious practice seeks to eliminate the mystical and emotional element in favor of some rigid intellectual or ethical system or in an effort to preserve intact some set of traditional institutional forms, it will remain as useless as a furnace cut off from its electrical source.

My theological upbringing, I realized, was like a one-legged stool, unstable and unreliable, because it emphasized the institutional dimension, harnessing the intellectual and the mystical elements so directly to tradition that creative thinking and genuine experience of God became practically impossible. I discovered that my devotional practice, including church worship, was driven mostly by duty and obligation and far less by love and affection. My relationship with God had been stunted, not by lack of effort but rather by misguided effort.

Instead of disclosing what God has already revealed to the world, and that in singular and orthodox fashion (that is, through dogma and creeds), what if we viewed the central purpose of religion as discovering how humans can relate to God? Wouldn't that task require a variety of approaches? As God cannot be confined to a single image or understanding, neither can human experience of God be one-dimensional. If contact with God is possible, then communication on many levels becomes essential. Every human being has a unique personality structure, and this uniqueness becomes

---

1. For von Hügel, religious tradition determines and defines patterns of worship, scripture, and orthodox belief.

important as a possible avenue to God. The New Testament expression of this is seen in the description of the church as the "body of Christ"—a unified organism that embraces incredible diversity; indeed, that depends upon diversity for its existence.

As individuals realize that they have their own unique way of interacting with the world, they will not attempt to force others into their mold. There is a place for each personality in the spiritual journey, a place for the religious thinker, the religious activist, the devotional practitioner, and the religious artist. There are many different ways of living the religious life and of experiencing God, each with its values, difficulties, and rewards.

How we conceive God determines how we experience God. Is God personal? The Christian tradition, as most religions, views God thus, with personal characteristics. Supernatural theism is unambiguously anthropomorphic. The natural language of meditation, devotion, and corporate worship is personal; we use this language regularly in our private devotional life and when we worship in church. There is nothing wrong with personifying God and addressing God as if God were a person.

Problems arise, however, when we literalize these personifications, as though "the right hand of God" means that God really has hands, and when God is said to speak, that God must have a larynx. Some years ago, a group of Baptists left the Texas Baptist Convention because they believed that God is male rather than female or sexless. Did they believe, I wonder, that God has male sex organs? If so, does God have to shave? Of course, such questions seem trivial, but they are not unimportant.

Perhaps we can ease some of the difficulty by a softer literalization of personal language for God, namely, by affirming that God is personlike. This means that God is separate from the universe, a living being separate from other beings and yet somewhat like us, though to a superlative degree. Nevertheless, literalizing these personifications leads to supernatural theism and the problems associated with it, such as the apparent contradiction between God's omnipotence, justice, and omnibenevolence. Human experience of God suggests that God cannot simultaneously be all-powerful, all-good, and all-loving, else there would be less injustice and tragedy in this world and more goodness and morality. Likewise, the biblical view of God can be an impediment to belief, for this God seems to display unattractive and even immoral behavior, displayed through qualities such as destructive anger, jealousy, and biased treatment of human beings. This God is depicted as choosing people selectively, fighting wars, defeating enemies, sending storms, plagues, and even death. Yet this God also heals the sick, spares the dying, and rewards goodness. Even normal human judgment condemns such behavior as inconsistent and immoral. In his publication *The Sins of Scripture*, Bishop Spong examines biblical moral principles attributed to the will of God and concludes that those who wish to base their morality literally on the Bible have either not read it or not understood it.

There are clearly problems associated with anthropomorphic personifications of God. Whatever God is ultimately like, whether personal, impersonal, or transpersonal (that is, more than personal), there are at least three dimensions of meaning to personal language of God that we need to retain:

- God's relationship to us is personal. It is doubtful that humans could worship something that does not have at least the status of personality.

- God has more the quality of "presence" than of nonpersonal "energy" or "force." To use language coined by the Jewish philosopher Martin Buber, God has the quality of a "Thou" rather than that of an "It," hence more the quality of a person than of an impersonal "source."

- God communicates with us, not necessarily audibly or by divine dictation, but God "speaks," sometimes through visions and dreams but also through "prodding" or "hunches." Vehicles for these can include other people, devotional practices, the scriptures of one's religious tradition, and daily circumstances.

As contemporary author Frederick Buechner advises, "Listen to your life. Listen to what happens to you because it is through what happens to you that God speaks." Paula D'Arcy states this truth more bluntly: "God comes to you disguised as your life."

Friederich von Hügel, valued more highly in his day as a spiritual director than as a theologian, found practical outlets for his significant intellectual skills. At the age of eighteen, sickened with typhus fever and left practically deaf, he embarked on a theological career. While he spent most of his life as a Catholic layman dedicated to theological and philosophical writing, at the age of forty he met the Abbé Huvelin, a distinguished spiritual director serving in a Parisian parish. Through his influence, von Hügel experienced a profound spiritual transformation that led him from his intellectual pursuits into the field of spiritual counseling, and it was as a guide and counselor that he made his greatest contribution.

Because of his deafness, much of his counsel occurred by correspondence, through the mail. Many of his letters exist in published form. Among those who sought his direction was Evelyn Underhill, distinguished in intellectual circles for her books on mysticism. Having the experience of a growing number of people who wrote to her for spiritual advice, she turned to von Hügel for help with her own spiritual formation. Because of her commitment to the mystical, experiential element in religion, she sensed an aversion to the institutional side of religion, particularly its historical and sacramental elements. Displaying a theocentric approach in prayer and worship, she belittled those who spoke of a relationship with Jesus or Christ, considering such attachment sentimental and unreal.

Sensing in her a tendency to go to extremes, either overemphasizing mystical (non-institutional) practices or their opposite, traditional (institutional) practices, von Hügel recommended moderation. Knowing "these two extremes to be twin sisters in such a soul as yours," he recommended the following minimal institutional plan: attendance at one church service on Sunday, with perhaps a midweek prayer meeting and one church-related retreat a year, coupled with a maximum of half an hour a day for private prayer and a three-to-five-minute examination of conscience at night before retiring. He also recommended the cultivation of some non-religious interest such as painting, music, or gardening, in addition to devoting two afternoons each week to visit the poor. This final option, he tells Professor Underhill, will do more than all the rest to blunt her intellectual religious bent and open her heart to the needs of all, and not only the audience of fellow intellectuals to whom her career had thus far been devoted.

More important than this, however, were von Hügel's efforts to get her to face the neglected side of the incarnational aspect in her religious life—of who Jesus Christ was and of what he revealed about God—making Christ's incarnation central to her thought and practice. From her writings, he knew she had a deep respect for Jesus, but this did not seem to carry through into her interpretation of Christianity or into her prayer life.

As a spiritual director, it was clear to von Hügel that there should be no coercion in the spiritual life. Dealing with a strong intellect, he believed that if his client did not face the neglected issue of the incarnation, there would be no spiritual growth. In her writings, she spoke often of what was mystical and symbolic in Christianity, but if she was to progress spiritually, she needed to become convinced, not of what ought to be real but of what in fact was historically real. Knowing her area of neglect, von Hügel asked her to consider changing her non-historical stance by acknowledging God's self-disclosure in Jesus Christ. If she could accept that much, not cognitively, by understanding it rationally, but by faith, then she could postpone decision concerning equally difficult yet ultimately less important items of belief such as the Virgin Birth and the resurrection.

Regarding her prayers, he proposed no sudden change in her theocentric approach, but asked whether she might at least admit that praying through Jesus Christ was a possibility. Perhaps she might admit that her way of praying, apophatically and to the Father alone, was one way but not the only way to pray. Could she continue praying as she felt led, yet introduce kataphatic images such as the Sea of Galilee and Calvary into her imagination? Such visualization might provide more credence to her understanding of the historical aspects of the incarnation. Such meditative prayer might also impact her understanding of God, help alleviate her doubt concerning the historical validity of Christianity, and increase her appreciation of God's presence in everyday life. It might also make her prayer more intercessory—more about others and their needs rather than exclusively about herself and her spiritual condition. Von Hügel's method served to draw her quietly yet progressively from her own self-sufficient efforts and merit to God's redemptive action through Christ, for only thus would she experience the transformation she desired.

After years of such direction, a new orientation emerged in Evelyn Underhill's life and writing. She did not convert to Catholicism, as some of von Hügel's directees did, but was drawn more deeply into her own Anglican tradition. Of von Hügel's advice she wrote: "I owe him my whole spiritual life, and there would have been more of it than there is, if I had been more courageous and stern with myself, and followed his direction more thoroughly . . . Until about five years ago, I never had any personal experience of Christ as Lord. I didn't know what it meant. . . . Somehow by his prayers and advice, he compelled me to experience Christ. . . . It took about four months—it was like watching the sun rise very slowly—and then suddenly one knew what it was."[2]

Devotional Practice

Christians speak regularly of God's love for humanity, but rarely about the importance of loving God. What does it mean to love God? Most of us are

2. Steere, *Spiritual Counsel and Letters of von Hügel*, 21.

familiar with the biblical injunction to love God with all our heart, soul, mind, and strength (Mark 12:30). It has been called the "greatest commandment." But what does it mean? Simply put, loving God means paying attention to God and to what God loves. It means "practice"—practicing the presence of God.

Modern Western Christians, particularly Protestants, have not made practice central. Other Christians, Roman Catholics and Eastern Orthodox, emphasize rituals and practice. So also Jews, especially Orthodox Jews, who pay great attention to the "way of Torah." Likewise, at the center of Buddhism lies the "eightfold path," centered on practice. Muslims carefully observe the "five pillars" of Islam, four of which are about practice. One pillar requires praying five times a day, a practice that takes about forty minutes. How different might Christians be if they spent forty minutes a day in prayer and meditation. Forty minutes of prayer a day can transform a person's life!

A major reason that Protestants pay little attention to traditional Christian practice goes back to the Reformation, which contrasted "faith" and "works." Protestants are "saved" by faith, not by works. To many Protestants "practice" sound like "works." But the point of practice is not to earn salvation by accumulating merit. Rather, practice is about paying attention to God. Practice is how we love God.

The notion that God can be known (or experienced) is foreign in the modern world and in much of modern theology. In skeptical theology, the reality of God or the sense of God's presence has been replaced by emphasis on ethics, that is, on behavior. Modern Christianity largely downplays mystical and relational notions of God, emphasizing instead the importance of "being kind" or "being good." In liberal theology, the highest virtue becomes a passion for justice. However, Christian practice historically has been about our relationship to both God and neighbor, about both God and the world, and not about choosing one over the other.

An encouraging sign of renewal in the church is the recovery of practice as central to the Christian life. If the Christian life is about relationship and transformation, practice will be central. By practice I mean all the things that Christians do together and individually as a way of paying attention to God. These include being part of a Christian community and taking an active part in its life, its worship, Christian formation, fellowship, and collective deeds of hospitality and compassion. In addition, they include devotional discipline, especially prayer and Bible study. Loving God also includes loving what God loves through the practice of compassion and justice in the world.

Like all relationships, life with God grows and deepens to the extent that we give it attention. It involves spending time in it, giving it thoughtful priority, and, ideally, enjoying it. Paying attention to our relationship with God matters because humans are ultimately relational. We don't first become ourselves and then have relationships. Rather, we are constituted by our relationships; they shape and form us. Likewise, paying attention to our relationship with God will shape us.

While many Christians enter Christianity through "conversion," they generally do not convert from another religion or from no religion at all. Rather, at some point they commit to a Christian way of life. Christian practice, essential to this process, transforms the deepest level of their being—the heart—and helps shape their Christian identity. The process of Christian identity and character formation leads from a limited identity to a larger identity, from a limited self to a larger self. This takes place through life "in Christ," and practice is how this happens. The Spirit of God works through practice. Practice is not simply something Christians do. Rather, practice nourishes them. This happens in corporate practice such as worship as well as through individual devotional practices. Christians are fed by practice.

Verbal Prayer

Like other spiritual practices, prayer is primarily about paying attention to God. There are three major types of Christian prayer: verbal prayer, meditation, and contemplation. Verbal prayer addresses God with words, whether audibly or silently, whereas meditation and contemplation are not about talking to God, but rather, listening for God.

There are five categories of verbal prayer: adoration or praise, thanksgiving, confession, intercession, and petition. The most common form of prayer, intercession and petition, focus on asking for something for ourselves or for others. This "wish list" approach requires an almost magical view of God—that God is an interventionist who sometimes answers prayer. Such a view of God is essentially untenable, for it presents insuperable problems.

For example, if God could have intervened to stop the Holocaust but chose not to, what kind of God would that be? Does it make any sense to think that God can intervene to stop terrorist attacks, or tornados from striking, or keep airplanes from crashing, but chooses (at least in some cases) not to? If so, why some and not others? And what about all the illness and tragedy that strike faithful believers? To suppose that God intervenes implies that God does so for some, but not for others.

Not only is the interventionist idea difficult in itself, but this idea of unanswered prayer is also problematic. Think of all the people who pray for safety and peace in time of war, or of those who pray for healing, and whose prayers are not answered. Yet we continue to pray in this fashion, and it seems right to do so, when it is practiced sincerely and maturely. For one thing, petitionary and intercessory prayer feel natural; they seem like a form of caring. In addition, we don't really know how prayer works. As we learn from physicians, prayers for the healing of others sometimes have unexplainable results, and perhaps other kinds of prayers do as well. While some healing might be psychosomatic—body and mind seem to be related in ways we do not fully comprehend—putting things in God's hands is beneficial. There is also the placebo effect. Trust increases expectation and reduces stress, both preconditions for healing and wholeness.

Regardless of their efficacy, petition and intercession, like adoration, thanksgiving, and confession, serve the central purpose of prayer. As previously noted, the goal of all prayer, including of meditation and contemplation, is intimacy. God isn't a vain emperor in need of worship and praise, nor does God need encouragement or sideline cheerleading. Even confession need not be demeaning or self-deprecating, in the sense of "I am so bad," or "here's where I have fallen short." Prayer is ultimately relational, about companionship. Even confession, when it is practiced, ought to be natural, like sharing thoughts about the day or concerns and desires for oneself and others with an intimate confidant.

Of course we might discuss prayer by thinking the obvious, namely, that God already knows about my day, but that misses the point. Out human nature is to share, for sharing is part of all intimate relationships. Our relationship with God deepens through disclosure and conversation. Like adoration, ultimately all prayer is a human way to love God.

Meditation

The second and third categories of Christian prayer are meditation and contemplation. While meditation is in vogue today, there is a difference between psychological relaxation techniques, Eastern meditational practices, and Christian approaches. Until recently, the Christian practice of meditation and contemplation occurred primarily in religious orders. Now they are being recovered by laity and clergy, Protestant and Catholic alike. What these practices have in common is that they do not involve talking to God, but rather listening for God. And they do so in different ways.

In recent years mind and brain science has discovered a greater understanding of the way our bodies and minds relate to each other. Meditation has been found to produce profound and largely positive effects upon both body and brain. As biofeedback training reveals, even average people can learn to control bodily functions that were once considered beyond conscious control.

In addition, meditational practice is known to produce remarkable psychological and physiological effects, bringing practitioners to deeper levels of brain functioning and to increased psychic awareness. Meditation and contemplation are known to produce alpha and sometimes theta waves, and in both of these states practitioners become more alert and perceptual ability may increase as the capacity of the mind changes. Physical reactions like blood pressure and heart rate, influenced by the mind, also become slower and steadier.

Meditation, a kataphatic approach to prayer, involves reflecting on an image, symbol, or phrase, sitting with it, holding it, remaining with it. A classic example is "Ignatian meditation," named after Ignatius of Loyola, the founder of the Jesuit order in the sixteenth century. This approach provides a structure for meditation on images in a biblical text. As we enter the text, the images of the text become means for God's Spirit to speak to us. Loyola's approach, recorded in his *Spiritual Exercises*, became the basis of the "Ignatian Retreat," a twenty-eight-day meditational retreat on the mission, life, passion, and resurrection of Jesus. By meditating on Christ's life and teachings, primarily through visualization exercises, participants are encouraged to become companions of the earthly Jesus, hence true and committed disciples of Christ.

In his *Study Guide for Celebration of Discipline*, Richard Foster provides a meditation on John 6—Jesus' feeding of the five thousand—that illustrates Loyola's meditational technique on scripture.[3] What follows is a paraphrase. Read the passage slowly, attempting to use all of your senses. Try to place yourself in the actual scene. Imagine yourself as the child who

---

3. Foster, *Study Guide for Celebration of Discipline*, 20.

give Jesus his lunch, or perhaps as one of the child's parents. Try to see the story—the hills, the faces of the people gathered about. Try to hear the story—the sound of the water, the noise of the children, the voice of Jesus. Try to feel the story, the hardness of the ground, the texture of your clothing. Finally, try to feel with your emotions—hesitancy at bringing your lunch, astonishment at the miracle of the multiplied food.

Then, in your imagination, watch the crowd leave and Jesus go up the hill. You are left alone. You sit on a rock and re-experience the events of the day. After a while, Jesus returns and sits on a nearby rock. For a time you are both quiet, looking out at the water and enjoying one another's presence. After a while, Jesus turns to you and asks, "What may I do for you?" Then you tell him what is in your heart, your needs, your fears, your hopes. When you have finished, you become quiet for a while. Then you turn to the Lord and ask, "What may I do for you?" And you listen quietly, prayerfully. No instructions are necessary, for you are just glad to be in Christ's presence. If words come, take them to heart. Often they will include practical instruction about some matter of life, for God wants us to live out our spirituality in the ordinary events of our days.[4]

Contemplation

Contemplation is a form of prayer based on internal silence. The purpose of contemplation is to sit silently in the presence of God. Many churches offer training in contemplative prayer, and in some areas one can find workshops on it.

As with meditation, find a quiet place, removed from any distractions, and initiate what will become for you a daily practice of sitting in silence (you can start with a span of two or three minutes, though eventually you will want to build to two sessions of twenty minutes each) to simply become aware of God's presence in your life. According to experts in stress reduction and pain management, two twenty-minute sessions of structured relaxation a day, utilizing activities such as meditation, deep breathing, yoga, or tai chi, can be as beneficial in reducing stress and restoring wellbeing as a two-hour nap. As it turns out, spiritual meditation achieves physical and emotional benefits while producing transformative spiritual results as well!

---

4. This approach to scripture is discussed more fully in chapter 8, in the segments on "Lectio Divina" and "The Four Senses of Scripture."

One of the most common forms of contemplation is called "centering prayer," associated especially with the Benedictine monk Thomas Keating. Through silence, the goal is to open your mind, and therefore your heart and entire being, to God. The goal is not to experience God directly, for as Keating reminds us, "God as He is in Himself cannot be experienced empirically, conceptually, or spiritually. [God] is beyond experiences of any kind. This does not mean that [God] is not *in* sacred experiences, but that God *transcends* them."[5] Nevertheless, sacred experiences lead us to the experience of emptiness, and the more one lets go, the stronger the presence of God becomes. Keating, one of Christianity's most reliable guides to meditation, put things into proper perspective when he cautioned that though all human beings are summoned into the presence of God by the fact of their birth, they become present to God only by their consent. "As our faculties and capacities to relate gradually develop and unfold," he noted, "the capacity to enter into new relationship with God increases, and each new depth of presence requires new consent. Each new awakening to God changes our relationship to ourselves and to everyone else. Growth in faith is growth in the right perception of reality."[6]

To get started, the following guidelines are indispensable. Begin by sitting comfortably, with your eyes closed. Sit in a straight chair, with your back erect and both feet flat on the floor. Rest your hands on your knees or thighs, palms up or down, whichever you find most comfortable. To calm yourself, take a deep, cleansing breath. Select a word or phrase that you will use throughout the period of silence; some possibilities include the words "joy, peace, love, grace, wisdom, unity, surrender, Christ, or Holy Spirit." It is helpful to choose a word or phrase that signifies your intent to consent to God's presence and action within. Of course, the sacred word you select is sacred not because of its meaning but because of its intent. It expresses your intent to consent to God, the Ultimate Mystery who dwells within you. Once you find a word or phrase you are comfortable with, try to stick with it. You may change words if you wish, but to avoid distraction, refrain from shopping around during the same period of prayer.

Sue Monk Kidd, a contemporary novelist, describes how this works. Having read *The Way of the Pilgrim*, the account of an anonymous Russian peasant in the nineteenth century who sought to pray the ancient "Jesus Prayer" ("Lord Jesus Christ, have mercy upon me") all day long, she decided

---

5. Keating, *Open Mind, Open Heart*, 17.
6. Keating, *Intimacy with God*, §1.

to use this as her centering prayer. She said it once, and then again, blending the prayer with her breathing as the pilgrim had done: "Lord Jesus Christ" on the in-breath, and "have mercy on me" on the out-breath. She repeated the prayer slowly, silently finding a rhythm that seemed to slow everything down, and this led her naturally to focus on Christ. As my centering prayer, I prefer to use phrases from the Lord's Prayer: "Thy kingdom come" on the in-breath, and "thy will be done" on the out-breath.

Because this time is dedicated to listening and reframing, Centering Prayer is not the time to pray consciously for others or for yourself. By consenting to God, you are embracing the past, present, and future, and the whole of creation. If you find a visual symbol to be more helpful than a verbal word or phrase, use it instead, but not as an object of meditation. Its sole use is to return you to silence whenever a conscious thought arises.

Another way to focus is to concentrate on your breathing, buoyed by its calming and rhythmic nature. As you do, taking slow, deep breaths, you will find it reducing stress and expelling other negative emotions lurking deep within. When thoughts intrude, gently return to your sacred word and focus on your breathing. As you practice regularly, the strength of habit will make it easier to let go of the normal flow of thoughts and distractions.

In our psyche there are obstacles to opening ourselves to God. As we quiet the mind, we discover various kind of thoughts arising from the stream of consciousness within. Some of these thoughts might be superficial, others insightful, and some may have emotional content. Some come from the unconscious, and may represent the consequences of traumatic emotional experiences stored in our bodies in the form of tension, anxiety, and various defense mechanisms. Ordinary rest and sleep do not get rid of them. But in interior silence and the profound rest that this brings to the entire organism, these emotional blocks begin to soften up, activating the natural capacity of the human organism to release things that are harmful. The psyche as well as the body expels material that is harmful to its health. When the unloading of the unconscious begins, many people feel that they are going backwards. If this happens, simply accept the emotion and continue the process. The practice will eventually bring about the necessary change of consciousness. Contemplative prayer is part of the whole process of integration, which requires opening to God at the level of the unconscious. Contemplation releases a dynamic that can be peaceful at times and at other times heavily laden with thoughts and emotion. Both experiences are part of the same process of integration and healing. Both are necessary to complete the process of transformation.

The goal of our practice is not contemplative prayer but the contemplative state, the permanent and abiding awareness of God that comes through the mysterious restructuring of consciousness. There will always be distractions in contemplative prayer. However, contemplative prayer is not on the level of thinking. It is consenting to God's presence in pure faith. Hence, the proper response to extraneous thought is to let it go. As Keating notes, "Do not resist any thought, do not hang on to any thought, do not react emotionally to any thought."[7]

Centering Prayer is not a duty and its goal is not proficiency. It is an exercise of intent, the cultivation of our will and our faculty of choice. During this time, our only activity consists in maintaining our intention to consent to God's presence and action. The ongoing journey then becomes whatever God wants it to be. If you are tempted to think that "doing nothing" for a period is invaluable, recall that no one hesitates to sleep at night. Practicing this prayer, however, whether in its abbreviated or lengthier version, is not doing nothing. It is a gentle form of activity, as long as the will keeps consenting to God. Returning to the sacred word or the act of breathing is enough activity to keep one awake and alert.

At the end of the chosen time span, slowly return to your ordinary world and thoughts. This may be a good time to converse with God or to refocus your thoughts. Take a minute or two before opening your eyes, because doing so suddenly can be uncomfortable. As your sensitivity to the spiritual dimension within develops with regular practice, you may begin to notice a heightened awareness of God's presence arising at times of ordinary activity. Keating likens this experience to the color added to a black-and-white television screen. The picture remains the same, but it is greatly enhanced. The color was present all along, but it was not transmitted because the proper receptive apparatus was missing. Centering Prayer is a way of tuning in to a level of reality that is always present and in which we are always invited to participate.

The sense of presence established during Centering Prayer has to be integrated with the rest of reality. If our method is effective, the presence of God becomes a kind of fourth dimension. It does not replace our three-dimensional world, but it becomes the most important dimension, that from which everything emerges and to which everything returns. The contemplative state

---

7. Keating, *Open Mind, Open Heart*, 99.

EXPERIENCING GOD THROUGH PRAYER, MEDITATION, AND SILENCE

is established when the circumstances of our life move from being experiences in themselves to an abiding state of consciousness.

While *In the Potter's Workshop* recommends an attitude of continued openness to God's presence, such an attitude must be undergirded by regular focused practice, a specific time each day for paying particular attention to God. For some Christians, this is a period of contemplative prayer. For others, it combines verbal prayer with Christian reading, primarily from the Bible but also from books of devotional readings. There are many sources of daily scriptural readings, some denominationally oriented but many nondenominational in nature. Among these are *Devotional Classics*, edited by Richard J. Foster and James Bryan Smith, *My Time with God*, edited by Amanda and Stephen Sorenson, and Frederick Buechner's *Listening to Your Heart*, a collection of brief readings for each day of the year.

During your daily practice, avoid reading for information or analysis, but rather read quietly, receptively, and unhurriedly. Daily practice is essential for both Christian formation and nourishment. A famous passage from the prophet Micah offers a compact expression of biblical faith. Micah asks, "What does the Lord require of you?" His answer: "To do justice, to love kindness, and to walk humbly with your God" (Micah 6:8). Christian practice is about walking with God, becoming kind, and doing justice. It is not primarily about believing certain things about God or about being a good person. Rather, it is about how one become a good person through the practice of loving God.

Desolations, "Dark Nights," and Depression

The spiritual world must be encountered through personal experience. However, experiential spirituality leads us into confrontations and encounters with the whole realm of spirit. Few people come away from this experience unscathed. We are wounded and can be transformed, but in the process, we come to know the "dark night of the soul." In our spiritual journey, there will be highs and lows, times when God is felt as deeply present, loving, guiding, and sustaining, and other times when we feel only the absence of God. Occasionally we may discover a state that seems devoid of all experience.

In psychotherapy, such events might be treated as problems to be solved. However, in the spiritual journey, we must guard against substituting consolation for desolation, bringing light into a "dark night," or working through feelings of God's absence, particularly since such experiences may be God's action. In the spiritual life, some conditions are to be "seen through" rather than "worked through." If a period of emptiness in prayer or in meditation can be attributed to some psychological block or to self-defeating behavior, we should try to correct it. However, if we discern that the emptiness is a natural and graced event in the course of spiritual growth, we should accept it. If we try to "produce" spiritual growth during periods of emptiness (or at any other time, for that matter), the result will be forced and end in frustration. Persistence in such behavior may well become destructive and lead to open anger toward God and even to alienation from God. This alienation is not the same as feeling anger toward God. We can be angry with another and still be loving and seek reconciliation. Alienation can lead to a rejection of previously held values and can disrupt one's relationship with God. While anger can be constructive, alienation is destructive.

In the natural course of spiritual growth, we need to distinguish between negative experiences of daily life—such as frustration, losses, and failures—and "dark night" experiences. "Dark nights" are deeper and more profound than any ups and downs of the natural or spiritual life. To be fully accurate, we should probably not think of the "dark night" as an experience at all, but rather as the deeper and ongoing process of unknowing. This may include loss of attachment to sensate gratification and to sensual aspirations and motivations as well as loss of previously construed faith understandings and of God images. Accompanying this can be loss of self-importance and of preoccupations about our self-image. In terms of the "dark night," we hardly think of "realization" in a normal way, for what is involved is more a subtraction of prior knowledge than an addition of new insight. The "dark night," then, is not so much an experience or a phase of development but rather the essence of one's ongoing spiritual journey, a current too deep and subtle to be identified. It may well appear that there is no worthy guidance in this drifting, that one is utterly dependent upon and abandoned to the unknown and unknowable essence of God. It is only through grace that we are blinded to the totality of this process and to our ignorance as to its ultimate implications. Where it otherwise, I suppose none of us would have the courage to embark upon this journey in the first place.

While the "dark night" process may include fear, grief, even despair, it is possible to differentiate our response to the "dark night" from psychological responses such as clinical depression. "Dark night" experiences are not usually associated with loss of effectiveness in life or work, as are depressions. Surprisingly, sense of humor is usually retained after "dark night" experiences. This humor is not cynical or bitter, as it might be in mild depression; rather it retains an effervescent quality. Finally, compassion for others is enhanced after "dark night" experiences. There is little or none of the self-absorption seen in clinical depression. Rather than feeling frustrated, annoyed, or resentful, people experiencing a "dark night" are more likely to feel graced and consoled.

Questions for Discussion and Reflection

1. In your estimation, is Christianity primarily about understanding God's revelation to humanity in biblical times, or is it equally about what God is saying or doing in the present? What are the advantages and disadvantages to each point of emphasis?

2. Do you tend to view God as personal, impersonal, or transpersonal? Can people worship God or relate to God meaningfully apart from a "personal" understanding of God? Explain your answer.

3. Describe the problems associated with supernatural theism. In your estimation, can they be resolved?

4. If Friedrich von Hügel is correct, that mature religion requires equal attention to the historical, mystical, and intellectual dimensions of faith, which area do you most emphasize, and which do you most neglect? Assess how this imbalance impacts your spiritual journey and your experience of God.

5. *For personal reflection*: If you favor emotional or mystical religious experience, what changes might you consider to achieve a greater balance with the historical or institutional side of religion?

6. *For personal reflection*: If you favor an intellectual or institutional approach to your faith, what changes might you consider to achieve a greater balance with the mystical or emotional side of religion?

7. Speaking specifically, how can Christians demonstrate their love for God effectively?

8. What forms of religious practice do you observe regularly? Are there other forms you would like to practice? If so, which, and why?

9. Of the five categories of verbal prayer, with which are you most familiar? In prayer, do you tend to emphasize the petitionary aspect? If so, which other types of prayer should you practice?
10. What problems are generally associated with an interventionist view of God? Should we stop praying to God in this manner?
11. Have you practiced meditation? If so, describe your experience.
12. What is your response to the idea of using the imagination in the way you pray?
13. What is your first reaction to contemplative prayer? Explain your answer.
14. Have you experienced the "dark night of the soul"? If so, how would you describe it? How long did it last? Did it produce any lifelong change? If so, explain your answer.

CHAPTER 8

Experiencing God through Worship, Community, and Scripture

The classical spiritual journey always begins elitist and ends egalitarian.

—Ken Wilber

To be honest, most of us are not Christians through chance or by conversion; most of us were born into Christian families and taken to church at an early age. Over time, many of us have consented to that faith tradition, affirming the religious choices made for us by our parents. Some of us still worship with the congregation of our birth, though most of us have moved and joined new churches. Others, unfortunately, have left church altogether and have rarely looked back.

Worship and Community

In my estimation, perhaps the single most important part of spiritual formation is to belong to a congregation that nourishes you even as it stretches you. Some of you may not be involved in a church and others may belong to one that leaves you dissatisfied or frustrated. If so, find a church that nurtures and deepens your Christian journey, that encourages worship with all of your being—body, mind, and spirit. Find one that worships a living Christ and a loving God. Of course, choosing a church is not primarily about feeling good, but church is meant to nourish us, not to make us angry or leave us bored. If your church worship is repetitive and unimaginative, if it feeds your mind but not your spirit, or if it is too noisy or judgmental, perhaps it is time to change.

The kind of Christian community that will nurture you depends upon your background and psychological temperament. Some Christians are nourished by sacramental and liturgical worship, some by more informed or contemporary worship, some by charismatic worship, others by great preaching or inspiring music, and still others by worship with lots of silence.

Authentic worship is profoundly subversive, for it affirms that God alone is the source of blessing, that God is Lord and the lords of this world are not. In worship we taste and see that the Lord is God. In worship we practice the presence of God, and we are nourished in mind and in spirit.

In contrast to the religions of the East, the Christian faith strongly emphasizes corporate worship. When Christians meet together, they often sense a profound unity, something they call *koinonia*, a deep inward fellowship in the power of the Spirit. One reason worship is a spiritual discipline is because it is an ordered way of living that gathers the faithful together so that God can transform them. True worship, then, is less an individual act and more a lifestyle. William Temple, Archbishop of Canterbury, defined worship as comprising a vast array of spiritual practices, including confession, contemplation, meditation, invocation, and surrender: "To worship is to quicken the conscience by the holiness of God, to feed the mind with the truth of God, to purge the imagination by the beauty of God, to open the heart to the love of God, to devote the will to the purpose of God."

Being part of a Christian community provides a setting for Christian education. This matters for both children and adults. Unfortunately, many children (and even some adults) are taught to read scripture literally, in ways that they will later need to unlearn. In a time of pluralism, multiculturalism, and rapid change, children and adults need to learn in ways that make sense in the twenty-first century, and not simply pass on outmoded teachings and techniques. It is difficult to give one's heart to something that one's head rejects.

In all world religions, the most common method of religious practice is participating in religious rituals or symbolic acts. Most humans are sacramental beings. They live and move symbolically and sacramentally. However, there is a problem with religious ritual, the temptation to celebrate these rituals as ends in themselves, without taking the next critical steps. The first is the importance of personal experience with God. Rituals are, after all, a means toward an end, and when that end is not kept in mind, the religious rites can easily become a form of idolatry. The answer to this dilemma, of course, is not to eliminate rituals, for human beings need to express their religious instincts in visible, audible, and other human ways. Rituals also allow us to express the indispensable communal dimension in worship. Because unselfish love is the essential element in religion, worship necessarily brings us closer to other people, and that needs to be celebrated by listening and singing together and by supporting one other in many different ways. On occasion, we need to be alone with God, but the fruit of that personal experience results in the second critical step, in our love and service toward others.

Authentic worship is profoundly transformative. To worship is to experience God, and to experience God is to love and serve others. Christian service involves two interrelated dimensions: love of God, manifested in worship, and love of neighbor, manifested in bringing joy to others and in addressing human need. Being part of a church creates opportunities for the collective practice of compassion and justice. These include caring for people within the church, outreach programs for people beyond the doors of the church, and advocacy of justice in our communities and in society at large.

Scripture

Christianity is centered in the Bible. Of course, it is ultimately centered in God, but it is the God of whom the Bible speaks and to whom it points. God may be known in other ways and through other religions, but to be Christian is to be centered in the God of the Bible. This is not a mark of Christian exclusion, but of Christian identity. The Bible is for Christians their sacred scripture, their sacred story.[1]

Yet the Bible has become a stumbling block for many. In the last half century, many Christians have left the church because of the Bible. More precisely, they left because the traditional literal way of interpreting the Bible, with its emphasis on biblical infallibility, historical factuality, and moral and doctrinal absolutes, became intolerable. In his writings, biblical scholar Marcus Borg provides an alternative to biblical literalism. Utilizing three adjectives—*historical*, *metaphorical*, and *sacramental*—he describes how scripture, creeds, and other normative Christian teachings should be understood.[2]

1. To speak of *the Bible as a historical product* is to see that it is a human product, not a divine product. Not "absolute truth" but relatively and culturally conditioned, the Bible uses the language and concepts of the cultures in which it took shape. It tells us how our spiritual ancestors saw

---

1. Borg, *Heart of Christianity*, 43.
2. Ibid., 43–60.

things, not how God sees things. The Bible is not verbally inspired, since the emphasis is not upon words inspired by God but on people moved by their experience of God.

For modern Christians, describing the Bible as sacred scripture and therefore as "holy" is to value the historical process known as canonization. The documents that make up the Bible were not "sacred" when they were written, but over time were declared sacred, meaning that they became the most important documents for that community, providing its foundation and shaping its identity.

2. Much of the language of the Bible is metaphorical: one-third of the Old Testament is poetry or semi-poetical literature. To speak of *the Bible as metaphor* is to emphasize that this language should not be interpreted literally. Metaphor does not mean that the Bible is not true, but rather that it is not primarily concerned with facticity. The Bible does contain history, but even when a text contains historical memory, its meaning is more than (not less than) literal. For example, although the exile in Babylon in the sixth century BCE really happened, the way the story is told gives it a more than historical meaning. It became a metaphorical narrative of exile and return, providing images of the human condition and its remedy. In other cases, as the Genesis stories of creation, there may be little or no historical factuality. Though these stories are not literally factual, they are profoundly true.

Because the Gospels combine memory and metaphor, some of these accounts, when literalized, become literally incredible. The story of Jesus changing water into wine at the wedding in Cana (John 2:1–11) illustrates the point. A literal reading of the story emphasizes the spectacular event as a sign of Jesus's identity, "proof" that he was divine. A metaphorical reading of this story yields a different meaning. It notes the story's literary context in John's Gospel as the opening scene of the public activity of Jesus. It seems to be John's way of saying: "Here in a nutshell is what the story of Jesus is about."

The story begins: "On the third day, there was a wedding." The phrase "on the third day" evokes the Easter story at the end of the gospel. The imagery of a wedding banquet helps us view the ministry of Jesus as a celebration at which the wine never runs out and the best is saved for last. Here we have a pointer to the sacramental nature of the Christian life and to the belief that Jesus is God's best.

A metaphorical reading of the Gospels provides rich meaning for Christians in all times and places; a literal reading misses all of this, emphasizing belief in the miraculous elements rather than on its meaning for a life of faith. Metaphorical language is *a way of seeing*. To apply this to the Bible means that in addition to its metaphorical language and metaphorical narratives, the Bible as a whole may be thought of as a "giant" metaphor. "Thus the point is not to believe in the Bible—but to see our lives with God through it."[3]

3. To speak of *the Bible as sacrament* is to say that it mediates the sacred. If a sacrament is a physical vehicle or vessel for the Spirit, the Bible is sacrament in the sense that it is a visible human product whereby God becomes present to us.

For modern Christians, "the Bible—human in origin, sacred in status and function—is both metaphor and sacrament. As metaphor, it is a way of seeing—a way of seeing God and our life with God. As sacrament, it is a way that God speaks to us and comes to us."[4] The Bible is a two-way bridge, a path to the divine and a way to connect to our deepest self. Like a backboard in the game of basketball, scripture is a means to an end, not an end in itself.

Lectio Divina

Devotional reading, whether from the Bible or from Christian classics, becomes another means to practice the presence of God. Reading devotionally, that is, meditatively and not intellectually, will become a means by which God speaks to us, challenging, convicting, and nourishing us. Unlike eating a meal routinely or hurriedly, this kind of reading is like savoring a particular morsel, like letting a slowly dissolving lozenge melt in your mouth. If we find something in our reading annoying or argumentative, simply dismiss it without a trace. In this case, disengaging the mind allows the spirit to flourish. This is time alone with God, not with a human author or someone else's agenda.

A meditational practice with a long history of practice in the Christian tradition is Lectio Divina, a simple yet profound way of praying the scriptures that transcends mental processing. Those who utilize this approach today emphasize a meditative, not a scholarly or literary approach, with the intention of learning what God has to say to us about the true meaning of life for themselves and for the world. In Lectio Divina one

3. Ibid., 57.
4. Ibid., 59.

works intensely with a short scriptural passage following four distinct steps called *lectio* (reading), *meditatio* (reflection), *oratio* (prayer), and *contemplatio* (contemplation). While these steps are usually presented as sequential, experienced practitioners often experience them as circular, with the steps unfolding in any order.

Following this method, participants are encouraged to select a text, reading it slowly and attentively. In the second step, known as *meditatio*, readers will engage with the text through focused mental reflection, using reason, imagination, memory, and emotions to work with the passage. The process may differ with each passage. Sometimes the passage may trigger a memory, or it might stimulate a thought or bring confusion. Participants might focus on a particular term, phrase, or compelling image. Another effective way of working with the text is to role play one of the characters. Whatever approach you use, this is not biblical research. This practice is not about acquiring information or scholarly perspective. It is about allowing the text to resonate with you own heart.

The third stage, *oratio*, encourages heart-to-heart encounter with scripture. As feelings arise, participants ponder them quietly, insightfully. If possible, feelings can be shaped into a prayer, using words of petition, gratitude, or concern. This is the moment when, in Paul's words, the Spirit begins to pray within you. A prayer, of course, doesn't have to be in words; the feelings themselves can be the prayer. If the text causes no such response, participants are encouraged not to force a response but simply to move on to the next step.

The final step is known as *contemplatio*, which in the mystical tradition denotes "resting in God." At this stage you suspend all mental and emotional activity and simply "rest" in the fullness of the experience. As with Centering Prayer, the real work goes on beneath the level of your conscious mind.

The practice of Lectio Divina may be summarized as follows:

- *lectio*: in your first reading of the text, listen for a phrase or word that stands out for you;
- *meditatio*: in your second reading, reflect on what impacts you, perhaps noting your responses in a journal;
- *oratio*: after reading the passage a third time, respond with a prayer or expression of what you have experienced or how you felt called to respond;
- *contemplatio*: after a fourth reading, rest in silence.

While *lectio, meditatio, oratio,* and *contemplatio* form the traditional sequence, experienced practitioners tend to follow the movement of the Spirit, weaving between the steps in a fluid way. Devoting half an hour a day to this practice, or even half an hour several times a week, will produce dramatic differences in your intimacy level with scripture. Words and images that arise during your time of *lectio* will percolate beneath the activities of your day, shaping what you see and do in remarkable ways. Incidentally, the passage you read need not be long. Some select a single sentence—even a single word—sometimes for days, until the text reveals its hidden treasure.

The question naturally arises as to where in the Bible you should begin to apply this method. While there is no correct answer to this question, two strategies are available. One is to pick a book of the Bible, such as the epistle of James, one of the Gospels, or a short letter by Paul, and simply begin. The Psalms are a perennial rich ground for Lectio Divina, as are Old Testament wisdom books such as Proverbs or Ecclesiastes. If you work at this process long and patiently enough, you may eventually cover the entire Bible.

The other strategy is to work with the daily lectionary. Many mainstream Christian denominations (Roman Catholic, Episcopal, Lutheran, Presbyterian, Methodist, and United Church of Christ) make use of a standard set of readings for Sunday and daily devotional use.[5] For each day, the lectionary provides several readings, including an Old Testament passage, an Epistle and a Gospel. You may choose any of these texts during your time of *lectio*, or else take the readings for the upcoming Sunday and work with them a bit at a time throughout the week: the Gospel one day, the Epistle the next, the Old Testament reading the next, or whatever approach you choose. The daily readings expand the range of biblical reading in worship and personal devotion by providing daily citations for the full three-year cycle of the Revised Common Lectionary. These readings complement the Sunday and festival readings. Thursday through Saturday readings help prepare readers for the Sunday ahead; Monday through Wednesday readings help readers reflect on what they heard in worship the previous Sunday. Again, the passage you read need not be long; it can be as short as a verse or even a single sentence or word.

While Lectio Divina is primarily done individually, group practice is becoming common. Group *lectio* can indeed be a powerful experience and a natural complement to group Centering Prayer. When practiced in

---

5. I recommend that you use the daily readings from the Revised Common Lectionary found online on the Vanderbilt Divinity library website.

a group setting, this exercise is very different from a Bible study group, for leaders and practitioners are not there to share or discuss or debate. A good way to proceed is to designate an appropriate leader, one who will adhere to the process. Following a period of silence, a designated person reads the scriptural passage, slowly and quietly. Before the actual reading, the leader instructs participants to listen for a sentence, phrase, or even a single word that seems to call for attention. After a moment of silence, the passage is read aloud again. Following this reading, the leader invites participants to speak aloud the word, phrase, or sentence that has moved them. Members of the group can be assured that repetition is appropriate, particularly since people often pick up different nuances in the text. After the exercise has run its course, the passage can be read a third time, followed by a return to silence for several minutes. The group leader may offer a closing prayer, after which the group leaves in silence.

While this group exercise focuses mainly on the first step of Lectio Divina, the silence between the readings provides participants space to engage in their own *meditatio* and *oratio*. Traditional fellowship and Bible study is well and good, but it tends to pull members back into their usual patterns of thinking, whereas this more meditative approach carries people "beyond the mind" into the greater "heart knowing" we have been exploring throughout this book.

What people gain from the slow, patient work in Lectio Divina is not only greater familiarity with scripture but also a distinct relationship with the text, described as the awakening of the unitive imagination, where the poetry of scripture and the poetry of one's own life come together to form a single whole.

Four Senses of Scripture

During the medieval period, the greatest amount of Christian writing was commentary on the Bible, for the Bible was viewed as a map of divine reality, as the means whereby ultimate reality was revealed to humanity. Presupposing that divine revelation was cryptic rather than clear, hidden behind the words and metaphors of scripture, medieval exegetes devised a hermeneutical method known as the "medieval quadriga," popularly known as the "four senses of scripture." This standard method of biblical reading, associated with Lectio Divina, followed a fourfold sense of interpreting scripture: (a) literal (reading a text naturally, at face value), (b) tropological (reading a text morally, as guidance for Christian conduct), (c), allegorical (reading a text in search of theological truth) and (d) anagogical (reading a text eschatologically, as futuristic hope).

The four senses are not four ways of analyzing a particular text rationally. They are four levels of listening to the same passage. This approach presupposes that scripture contains a mysterious dynamic that moves one to ever deeper levels of understanding the Bible as Word of God. While modern exegetes focus on the literal sense of scripture, seeking out the meaning of words and the cultural background of a text, this is not our purpose. The method of Lectio Divina is not done for the sake of information but for insight, not to learn something but rather to encounter Christ and develop a friendship. The goal of the process is to rest in the presence of God, not to learn something new about scripture.

Before printing was invented, there were only a few manuscripts of the Bible available. Monks would read one book of the Bible, such as Isaiah or one of the Gospels, for an entire year. They were expected to memorize scripture so that they could run blocks of scripture through their memory all the time. They would start reading, and when something struck them, they would stop, reflect on the text, then pray over it. Monks might spend most of the time with just one or two words, resting in the presence of God. The whole monastic environment, steeped in scripture, encouraged such meditation and contemplation.

Unfortunately, much modern-day reading, if it is done at all, focuses on speed-reading and on consumption of information. What most people want today are summaries and soundbites, breaking news and headlines. *Lectio* is just the opposite. It requires reading slowly, savoring a text. What is remarkable about *lectio* is that the reader moves from one level of scripture to the next seamlessly, from one level of relating to God to another simultaneously. Gradually, as friendship with God deepens, the four senses of scripture begin to unfold as a dynamic within one's life. As we read sacramentally, chewing and digesting each word, we find the Word of God—the Logos—deep within us, not dormant and lifeless, like a statue, but living and dynamic. Paraphrasing John 6:56, "those who gnaw my words and savor my message abide in me, and I in them."

How does this dynamic work?[6] The first, or literal, sense of scripture is the historical message and the example of Jesus. When we engage scripture through Lectio Divina, we begin to put what it says into practice. Only

---

6. The remainder of this segment is adapted from Keating, *Intimacy*, 97–100.

by practice do we understand it. In practice we reach the second sense, the moral level. As we interiorize scripture and put it into practice, we find ourselves moving beyond the moral sense into the third level, the allegorical realm. We become aware that the events of scripture are about us, mirroring our life in its pages.

Thomas Keating recalls the time when his spiritual director encouraged him to read the entire Old Testament. He was more interested in other spiritual classics, but he agreed to the assignment. He started with Genesis, and by the time he got to Exodus, a new understanding of the text began to emerge. The words started jumping out at him, and he grew excited. As he read how the Israelites crossed the Red Sea, abandoning their former way of life, and then as they began murmuring against their leader, he felt he was reading his own story. A few words set off huge vistas of meaning and understanding, and from that point on, scripture reading became exiting and relevant. This is what the allegorical sense of reading does. It becomes a mirror into your life, enabling you to identify your own spiritual journey with the events of scripture. Salvation history, available in the sacraments, through scripture, and accessed through prayer, is the same grace at work. At the allegorical level, believers begin listening to the voice of God speaking through the liturgy, through Lectio Divina, and in the events of their own lives. When you reach this level, you read scripture differently. No longer simply historical documents, they become stories about one's own experience of the spiritual journey. As seekers identify with the texts of scripture, they begin to confront the darker side of their personality, the repressed areas of their ego that subconsciously thwart their growth and openness to the divine.

The allegorical level of scripture involves confronting the pain and emotional baggage in our unconscious—all the damage done since we were born. As we break through this protective psychological wall, with the help of contemplative reading and prayer, we still need to undergo the purgation or purification of all the unconscious baggage. This baggage—useless trash—must be discarded before the unitive experience can take place. The unitive experience occurs when our thoughts and actions are motivated by our true self rather than by the false self, with its excessive demands and hidden agendas. The fourth sense of scripture, the anagogical or unitive level, represents a phase where the seeker is so immersed in scripture that the Word of God comes alive in and through him or her as a kind of continuing revelation.

There is a spiral movement of the four senses of scripture. As you return to the same passage in scripture, it begins to take on new meaning. As you interiorize the four senses of scripture in your life, you come back to the same texts, only at a deeper level of understanding. This spiral motion is the way all aspects of the contemplative life develop. It is not that scripture has changed, but that you have changed. That's the transformation God wants to perform in our lives.

What moves us from one level to another is not something we do or some insight we gain. According to the method of Lectio Divina, we just keep reading. As we listen we grow in trust and in love, as in any relationship. The Spirit who inspired scriptures will enlighten us concerning its meaning. Scripture is ultimately addressed to our inmost being. It starts with what is most outward and moves toward what is most inward, in order to awaken us to the abiding presence of God. This final stage of *lectio*—resting in God—is often left out of scripture reading. Nevertheless, it is the purpose of all the other stages, and the ultimate purpose of life.

Questions for Discussion and Reflection

1. Do you prefer formal or informal forms of worship? Explain your answer.

2. Overall, what has been your experience in church worship? Do you find regular participation in church life to be necessary for Christian formation? Explain your answer.

3. What role does imagination play in your spiritual life? What is your favorite Christian movie, novel, or band? Explain your choices.

4. What do Christians generally mean when they say that the Bible is "holy"? Explain your answer.

5. What does it mean to view the Bible as both metaphor and sacrament? Describe the value of a metaphorical way of reading scripture. How can metaphorical ways of understanding scripture be considered sacramental?

6. Why did medieval Christians introduce the idea of the "four senses of scripture"? How are these related to Lectio Divina?

7. What has been your experience with reading and studying the Bible? Do you tend to read for information, for self-understanding, or as a way to relate to God?

CHAPTER 9

Experiencing God through Pain, Suffering, and Loss

> Where you stumble and fall, there you find pure gold.
>
> —Carl G. Jung

SUFFERING IS A UNIVERSAL condition, and there is no way to avoid it. There is hardly a time in any family when someone is not experiencing significant illness or when that family has not experienced the loss of a loved one. Life and death are part of a continuum, and whatever is alive is moving toward death. In some cases death comes suddenly, but generally speaking, all living things are in the process of dying. Pain, suffering, and loss are part of that process.

Illness seems to affect children and the aged more than the rest of the population, and for obvious reasons. On the whole, children are acquiring an effective immune system, and childhood illnesses benefit that process. Likewise, the elderly are more susceptible to illness because their immune system is less functional than before. People with healthy genes, a good immune system, and a positive mental attitude often seem to thrive; others are not so fortunate.

There are things most of us can do to mitigate the effects of suffering and pain, such as diet and exercise, but that is not the subject of this chapter. Our focus will be on accepting pain and suffering when they come—not by welcoming it or by exaggerating its effects through hypochondria—but by using its mentoring power beneficially.

In Old Testament times, suffering due to sickness and tragedy was believed to be caused by sin. People either assumed or were taught that suffering was God's punishment for disobeying divine laws (see Deut. 28:27–28). Of course, this belief is not that of present-day Judaism. However, even within the Old Testament we find objections to the notion that sickness is

EXPERIENCING GOD THROUGH PAIN, SUFFERING, AND LOSS

the result of sin. The strongest protest is found in the book of Job, which provides three explanations for suffering. The first attempt to explain suffering appears in the prologue: (a) *innocent suffering arises from arbitrary divine decisions.* Job is but a pawn in a heavenly challenge, and humans are unwitting victims. Job's friends propose a different interpretation: (b) *suffering is due to sin*; hence Job's suffering is deserved. Job's own experience, and the reader's knowledge of the situation, invalidate this conclusion. (c) *The Creator of all things must be the cause and source of suffering.* According to Job, humans suffer because God is capricious and unreliable. In the divine speeches, God merely ignores Job's questions, changing the subject from Job's pain to the creation of the cosmos.

In the past, the customary way of understanding suffering, as punishment for sin, seems validated by Job's "repentance" in 42:6. Recent biblical and theological study has led to more viable explanations, including viewing suffering as:

1. *A test of one's character and integrity.* The prologue itself tells us that God allowed Job's misfortunes to befall him so that Job's integrity might be tested (2:3). Elsewhere in the Bible God is said to test individuals, such as when Abraham was told to sacrifice his son Isaac (Gen. 22:1). While experiences certainly test our character, we must add that in Job's case he never regarded his misfortune as a test.

2. *A source of moral discipline.* In the book of Job, Elihu claims that pain and sickness sometimes act as warning against sin and as a defense against pride and complacency (33:15–33).

3. *Vicarious suffering.* This view is depicted in the Suffering Servant poems in the book of Isaiah, particularly in 52:13––53:12, interpreted by Jews as reference to Jewish Diaspora experience and by Christians as a reference to Christ's atoning sacrifice on the cross. Such suffering is said to be an instrument whereby God's will is accomplished, bringing blessing to the world.

4. *A place of encounter with God.* As in Job's case, God can be experienced either as absent or as particularly close and available in suffering and pain.

5. *An impersonal result of universal sin.* In the Bible, this is how death seems to be understood, as a sort of karmic effect of cosmic rebellion and human wrongdoing (Rom. 6:23). The Christian doctrine of

"original sin," which views Adam's sin as having infected all humans, is sometimes introduced as a variant of this explanation.

6. *A Mystery*. Innocent suffering is simply beyond human comprehension. Ultimately no one can give Job an adequate explanation for his suffering. Only God knows, though people of faith expect that one day all will become clear.

In biblical times, Greeks and Romans held a traditional understanding of sickness, viewing it as the direct result of the anger of the gods against human beings who had violated natural laws. People born blind, for example, or who contracted diseases such as leprosy, were considered cursed by God and were shunned by most people. This idea was propagated by the majority of Christians throughout history, and it continues to be held in some circles to this day.

Although some illness may be caused by moral and religious failure, we must note that in his ministry Jesus contravened all notions that God brings sickness or pestilence upon people because of divine wrath. Jesus' healing ministry embodies the exact antithesis of this idea. Before healing people, Jesus did not inquire whether they were bad or good or whether they had repented or were reforming. He loved people as they were, and desired only to help them out of their misery.

Another idea current in Christian circles today is that God sends illness or deprivation upon believers for their good, or to accomplish divine ends. Speaking of the value of illness, they sometimes point to the "thorn in the flesh" passage in 2 Corinthians 12:7–10, where Paul speaks of a malady in his life sent to keep him humble. The passage includes the oft-quoted words, "My grace is sufficient for you, for (my) power is made perfect through weakness." When we examine this passage, however, we note that Paul is not attributing the malady to God, nor is he indicating that it was a good thing. Rather, the malady "came as a messenger of Satan" to keep Paul humble. Self-centeredness itself is a malady, when it prevents us from being God-centered. No doubt God would have preferred Paul without his pride *and* his thorn, but the point of the passage is that suffering for one's faith can bring God glory: "Therefore I am content with weaknesses, insults, hardships, persecution, and calamities for the sake of Christ; for whenever I am weak, then I am strong" (2 Cor. 12:10).

Ultimately, it is a travesty to blame God for suffering. While a loving God can use the afflictions of evil to work good, a loving God does not send evil. Some suffering redeems, but most suffering destroys. God wills life, not death; healing, not disease. The essence of God's manifesto regarding good is found in the Beatitudes (Matt. 5:3–12). There we learn that God's desire is to bless and not curse, to grant wholeness and not deprivation.[1]

One of the greatest lessons I have learned as a Christian is that nothing befalls us without first going through God. In other words, when we suffer, God suffers with us. Perhaps for this reason, Brother Lawrence writes that God seems "nearer to us, and more effectually present with us, in sickness than in health."[2] Often, when things go well, we become self-sufficient and oblivious of God, but when illness and tragedy strike, we recognize our vulnerability and our need of help. The good news is that God is especially near at such times, willing and able to help. As environmentalist Wendell Berry once said, speaking at a coffeehouse on a dreary December day, "It gets darker and darker, and then Jesus is born." Annie Dillard pushed the imagery deeper when she writes, "If you want to look at the stars . . . darkness is required."

Christianity is the only faith that looks squarely at the almost limitless extent of human agony and suffering, takes it seriously, and then offers meaning, redemption, and victory. This view is best depicted in Jesus' resurrection. The essential message of the teaching, life, death, and resurrection of Jesus is that evil and death have been defeated, and that we share in that victory. As the incarnation makes clear, God is with us in our joys and in our trials. Christianity neither ignores human agony nor dismisses it as irrelevant.

Essential to the biblical doctrine of creation is the notion that God created human beings for fellowship. Love created human beings, and that love remains with God's creatures for the long haul, through thick and thin. As the apostle Paul proclaimed, "If God is for us, who is against us? . . . . Who will separate us from the love of Christ? Will hardship, or distress, or persecution, or famine, or nakedness, or peril, or sword? . . . No, in all these things we are more than conquerors through him who loved us. For I am convinced that neither death, nor life, nor angels, nor rulers, nor things present, nor things to come, nor powers, nor height, nor depth, nor anything else in all creation, will be able to separate us from the love of God in Christ Jesus" (Rom. 8:31–39).

---

1. The Beatitudes are discussed more fully in the epilogue.
2. Lawrence, *Practice of the Presence*, 55.

There are many ways we can keep in touch with the Easter victory, ways of opening our lives to the spiritual dimension. These include prayer, sacrament, meditation, and contemplation. There are also qualities such as faith, humility, and courage that are central to the victorious and fulfilled life. However, there is yet another way to encounter the deep truths of the gospel. We can make contact with the risen Christ through a language far older than logical or conceptual thinking— through the faculty of imagination, the language of images, feeling, and love. Imagination can lead to atom bombs and can be used for evil or escapist purposes. However, imagination can also open us to the realm of the divine, to the loving, conquering, resurrected Jesus, who is able to sympathize with our weakness because he was tested as we are, perfected through suffering (Heb. 2:10; 4:15).

Creative Suffering

Life is beautiful, but it is also hard—for all human beings, but even harder in misfortune or deprivation. While life is harder for some than for others, in everyone's life there is a mixture of privilege and deprivation. Every event bears pain and joy; our response determines our growth, physically, emotionally, and spiritually.

In *Creative Suffering*, Swiss physician Paul Tournier demonstrates persuasively that many of the world's greatest statesmen, religious leaders, creative artists, and physicians suffered great loss and deprivation in their early years. Deprivation, it seems—whether due to failure, loss, accident, bereavement, or infirmity—has the power to transform lives. This is true not only in the lives of individuals but also of nations. Sociologists indicate that the most propitious regions for the development of civilization are not the tropics, or areas where the weather is most favorable, but rather those regions with the greatest contrast in climate. Such extremes release a surge of creativity, and it is this creative reaction to life's extremes that influences change, vitality, and development. Consider also what happened to the two most important countries defeated in World War II, Germany and Japan. Both responded with prodigious development, as epitomized by Emperor Hirohito when he announced surrender: "We must now accept the unacceptable, and surmount the insurmountable." A nation's value, like a person's, can be measured not so much by success as by how it responds to failure or defeat.

EXPERIENCING GOD THROUGH PAIN, SUFFERING, AND LOSS

As I learned recently while recovering from a prolonged ailment, when exercising an injured or debilitated area of the body, it helps to focus on the parts of the body that are working well, and not solely on the parts that are incapacitated. Likewise, speaking spiritually, when you suffer deprivation, focus on blessings rather than on woes.

Positive, creative, reactions to suffering enhance one's life; negative, resistant, reactions stunt it. Like a game of chess, a single move can change the entire game. Think also of the "snowball effect": every positive reaction renews hope and enhances progress, and every negative reaction paves the way for further defeat. Also helpful in this respect is to imagine a watershed. In Pennsylvania, where I live, two drops of rain fall side by side. One makes its way to the Atlantic Ocean via the Chesapeake, the other to the Gulf of Mexico via the Ohio and Mississippi rivers. As with a tunnel, there are two ways out, one backward and the other forward; one leads to progress, the other to calamity.

Two beneficial outcomes exist in every illness: the possibility of healing and of personal growth. In both cases, the attitude of faith makes a huge difference. Patients, generally speaking, think only of healing, and that is normal. When you are in need of healing, go to the doctors, where you will get professional help. But go also to God, for while doctors seek to heal the whole by healing the part, God, it seems, heals the parts by healing the whole. All healing, however, ultimately comes from God, since God is creator of the natural as well as the supernatural, the physical as well as the spiritual.

In *On Death and Dying*, Swiss psychiatrist Elisabeth Kübler-Ross described the five stages in acceptance of grief or loss. At first there is shock, when a patient learns or assesses the severity of illness or the death of a loved one. Shock is accompanied by denial—unwillingness to accept the loss. This is followed by the "bargaining stage," as if the patient could placate fate or God through submission. During the fourth stage, the feeling of helplessness leads to withdrawal and sometimes to harmful self-medication. Finally, after a long pilgrimage, the sick person or mourner arrives at peaceful acceptance.

With variations, we can see Kübler-Ross's stages in those who advance to old age—some people remain in good health until the end, but most people experience physical and mental decline. For those who age graciously, that is, who reach the stage of acceptance, the greatest factor is faith. Retirement and old age are forms of deprivation—loss of prestige, of social relationships, of routine—but also opportunities for personal growth. Those who find meaning in retirement generally find it through creative transformation; these people become embedded in the moment, living mindfully. This requires new values and fresh inspiration.

When Jesus spoke of discipleship, he talked about renunciation and loss of the old self. His words ring true, because he accepted the cross, despite undergoing inner struggle at Gethsemane (Matt. 26:36). Struggling with loss and deprivation is part of discipleship, because every trial brings us closer to faithfulness and thus to Christ. It is in suffering that we perceive his nearness, his presence, his participation in our lives. In the end, it is not simply human acceptance of suffering or loss that matters, but God's love that makes acceptance possible and leads us forward. According to Tournier, "I believe we can face everything when we believe we are loved."[3]

Like most families, mine was not spared traumatic, life-changing calamities. At the age of ten, my father lost an eye in a sledding accident, and at the age of forty-eight, while in the prime of her life, my mother contracted cancer. It was breast cancer, quite possibly a woman's worst fear, and it struck while my mother was fully engaged in a care-giving ministry for the God she loved and served. A mastectomy was performed, and after several months of improving health, she discovered another lump forming in her other breast. Was this spreading of cancer an indication that her ministry, perhaps even her life, was at an end, or was this experience a "wound of love," like the limp that the Old Testament patriarch Jacob received when he wrestled with God, when he received a new name (Israel) and a renewed promise for himself and his progeny?

This event came at a time when my parents experienced a deepening of their faith and an enlarging of their ministry. My mother would go on to live forty additional years as a cancer survivor. My father became ordained to the gospel ministry in 1966, two years before his retirement, and he spent the next twenty-five years teaching himself Greek and Hebrew, eventually reading the entire Bible in the original languages, something few seminary graduates or Bible scholars have accomplished. And he did this with the use of one eye.

As a young adult, discouraged and downhearted, I confronted my parents with a litany of doomsday scenarios. Without a moment's hesitation, my mother responded out of the reservoir of hope that had fueled her faith during times when her life was at risk, particularly as a missionary in

---

3. Tournier, *Creative Suffering*, 90.

Colombia—the Syria, Iraq, and Afghanistan of its day in the sense of deep sectarian violence and conflict and the place that inspired Fidel Castro to become a militant Marxist. My mother's response as I confronted my fears was hopeful and unwavering: "The best is yet to come." She knew, quoting Corrie ten Boom, the Dutch Christian who survived the concentration camps where she was sent for harboring Jews during World War II, that "There is no pit so deep that God's love is not deeper still."

While most suffering and deprivation is borne individually, with the help of others, some deprivation may be redemptive or vicarious. In ancient times, the people of Israel viewed the Babylonian exile as divine punishment for social injustice and religious unfaithfulness. That, at least, is the interpretation given in Israel's prophetic literature. However, an alternative interpretation arose, based on the book of Job. According to this view, Job is Israel, and the story of Job an allegorical account of Israel's experiences during the Babylonian exile. This interpretation views Israel as an innocent victim, and the exile as the story of servant Israel's vicarious suffering on behalf of the nations of the world, including Israel's unrighteous enemies. Such an interpretation became useful to Christianity's characterization of Jesus as the Suffering Servant of the Lord, as the one who's suffering would bring salvation not only to Israel but also to the Gentiles (see Isa. 49:1–7 and 53:1–12). According to Isaiah 53, the Servant's suffering is not for his own wrongdoing but is the way he brings his people to salvation.

While there are many ways to understand suffering, one is to view it as having redemptive value. In this perspective, one's suffering is offered as a prayer for the common good. In redemptive suffering, we stand with others in their pain and suffering. There is an active and a passive role here. The passive side involves those trials that enter our daily lives. These can be minor or tragic. Sometimes they come through disobedience or poor choices. Other times we are caught in the riptide of a good world gone bad—a bad economy that endangers our life savings, unemployment, an illness or accident that changes our life forever. When we suffer things for which we are not responsible and over which we have no control, we are to endure them patiently, putting our trust in God.

We can also offer our sorrows and suffering as gifts to God, asking that they be used to heal the world. The active side of suffering involves standing in solidarity with people in need, voluntarily taking into ourselves the griefs and sorrows of others in order to set them free. In this process, we need not persist into co-dependence, shouldering indefinitely the burdens of those unwilling to change. Rather our role, like that of the Good Samaritan, is to offer a hand-up to those in genuine need, not a handout to panhandlers.

The Face We Had Before We Were Born

Modern Western society presents a rosy picture: the journey ahead is upward and onward. You can be successful, and you can do it by yourself. Jesus, however, presents us with a different model, that of death and resurrection—a pattern of renewal, of daily dying to self. This leaves us with an important question, "How much false self are we willing to shed to find our true self?" The true self is who you are from the beginning, in the heart of God, the "face we had before we were born," as the Zen masters say. In this light, Carl Jung offered a momentous insight: "Life is a luminous pause between two great mysteries, which themselves are one."

Sometimes the end is the beginning, and the beginning points toward the end. Agreeing with Jung, we can affirm that the One Great Mystery is revealed at the beginning and forever beckons us toward its full realization. Many of us cannot let go of this implanted promise. Some call this homing device their soul, some call it the indwelling Holy Spirit, and others think of it as nostalgia or dreamtime. Whatever we call it, we cannot ignore it. It calls us both backward and forward, to our foundation and our future at the same time. The soul lives in such eternally deep time.

Speaking of this mystery, Richard Rohr notes that we are called forward by "a kind of deep homesickness," an inherent dissatisfaction that comes from our original and radical union with God.[4] Like loneliness, sadness, and depression, sickness, loss, and deprivation can serve as beacons to light our way home. One of the reasons the Wizard of Oz has such lasting appeal is because Dorothy is guided forward to Oz and back to Kansas by her constant love and desire for home. Restlessness and dissatisfaction in life can serve as pointers to our destiny in God. The moment that we find ourselves in the presence of God is the moment we also find ourselves inside God.

The end was planted in us at the beginning, and it gnaws at us until we get there freely and consciously. Suffering, tragedy, and all episodes of loss in our lives are potentially sacramental. As Jung put it, "when you stumble and fall, there you find pure gold." God hides, and is found, precisely in

4. The material in this segment is adapted from Rohr, *Falling Upward*, 65–96.

EXPERIENCING GOD THROUGH PAIN, SUFFERING, AND LOSS

the depths of everything, especially so in the deep fathoming of our pain, suffering, weakness, and failure. This "something real" is what all the world religions point to when they speak of heaven, nirvana, bliss, or enlightenment. Their only mistake is to push it off into the next world. "If heaven comes later, it is because it is first of all now."[5]

How does God operate? We really don't know. But so many have encountered God in their weakness that we realize God's strength is God's ability to be patient, to refrain from overt use of power. From our perspective, then, we can say that God is a god of weakness, acting as much by persuasion as by direct action.

In tragedy and sickness, we are no longer in charge. That is good news, because all attempts to engineer or plan our own enlightenment are doomed to failure, since they are ego driven. The ego's job is to protect the status quo, so failure and humiliation force us to look beyond our comfort zones. Thus, we must stumble and fall. We must get out of the driver's seat for a while or we will never learn how to give up control to our soul's True Guide.

In the spiritual world, we do not really find something unless we first lose it, choose it, long for it, and personally find it again—only now on a new level. In Luke 15 we find three parables about losing something—a sheep, a coin, a son—searching for them anew, and finding them once again. This new appreciation is followed by the kind of sincere celebration that comes with any new realization.

If you desire to grow spiritually, eventually some idea, event, or relationship will enter your life that you are not equipped to handle, using your present skill set. Richard Rohr calls such a situation a "stumbling stone," an event that causes you to leave your comfort zone in life.[6] Often such an experience involves physical or mental suffering. In this case, suffering will not solve any problem mechanically so much as it discloses the chronic problem in our lives, the refusal of our ego to let go. In such cases, suffering has a mentoring role, that of opening up new spaces within us for learning and loving. Francis of Assisi noted that when he kissed the leper, "what had been nauseating to me became sweetness and life." He marked that moment as his conversion, as the defining moment in his life, when he tasted his own insufficiency and began drawing from a different source.[7]

---

5. Rohr, *Falling Upward*, 95.
6. Ibid., 68.
7. Ibid., 69–70.

I am currently undergoing treatment for a condition diagnosed as Parsonage-Turner Syndrome (PTS). A rare disorder, also called brachial neuritis, its cause and treatment are largely unknown. It has become my "stumbling stone," unlike any I have experienced. The onset of the disorder, now in its sixth month, required the alignment of three factors to create a "perfect storm" in my upper body: (1) a physical disposition or susceptibility to the syndrome; (2) physical distress caused by overuse of the shoulder, arm, and pectoral muscles; and (3) the presence of a trigger mechanism, in my case, a viral attack. The syndrome began suddenly, with shoulder pain that rapidly amplified in severity and intensity. The shoulder pain led to progressive motor weakness, numbness, partial muscular paralysis, and physical abnormalities in the shoulder and upper back.

The disorder initially left me weakened and dizzy, causing falls due to fainting spells. For an entire month, I was unable to sleep. Eventually, the syndrome gravitated to my right shoulder, then to my middle and lower back. Doctors, physical therapists, a myofascial specialist, and a chiropractor examined me, with differing diagnoses. After various hospitalizations, doctors' visits, and unpleasant tests, I was eventually diagnosed with PTS, though the experts disagreed on my rehabilitation regimen. Due to widespread denervation, muscle strength imbalances, and an unstable back, I am still unable to perform specified exercises.

Short-term prognosis is guarded, due to nerve damage, although long-term functional recovery seems hopeful; 89 percent of patients recover fully after three years. Thankfully, my energy and mobility are returning, but progress is slow. I no longer get fatigued, and sleep is becoming more normal.

I believe God has much to teach me through this illness. I have already learned a great deal about myself, about God's elusive nature, and about how better to tap into divine resources. Undoubtedly, there is more learning and growing ahead, probably more than I can achieve in one short lifetime, making the notion of eternal life increasingly plausible. While increasing my hope for healing, this illness has increased my patience and given me a deeper appreciation for family and strangers, in whom I increasingly find the image of God. With Anne Lamott, I am discovering that "when God is about to do something wonderful, God always starts with a hardship, and when God is going to do something amazing, God starts with an impossibility."[8] Von Hügel's final words, written to his niece, fittingly

---

8. Lamott, *Plan B*, 33–34.

summarize life: "Remember, no joy without suffering, no patience without trial, no humility without humiliation, no life without death."[9]

What von Hügel learned at eighteen from his own spiritual director, Father Raymond Hocking, when he decided on a career in theology, he applied as a spiritual counselor: "You want to grow in virtue, to serve God, to love Christ? Well, you will grow in and attain these things if you will make them a slow and sure, but utterly real, mountain-step plod and ascent, willing to have to camp for weeks in spiritual desolation, darkness, and emptiness at different stages in your march and growth. All demand for constant light, all attempt at eliminating or minimizing the cross and trial, is so much soft folly and puerile trifling."[10] These words reflect what Jesus taught his followers about the cost of discipleship: "If any want to become my followers, let them deny themselves and take up their cross and follow me. For those who want to save their life will lose it, and those who lose their life for my sake and for the sake of the gospel, will save it" (Mark 8:34–35). A more realistic description of the Christian spiritual journey has not been recorded. But the story does not end here, for Jesus also teaches his followers that wherever they go, he will accompany them (Matt. 28:20). Those who are yoked to Jesus experience exhilaration and joy daily, even in times of trial, for Christ's burden is light (Matt. 11:30).

Courage: Our Finest Hour

Is it possible for those victimized by deprivation or great misfortune, such as the physically and mentally disadvantaged, to discover in that experience creative energy? Tournier answers that question affirmatively, but only if two conditions are present: (a) they must find a task in life and the tools to perform it adequately, and (b) they must learn to tap into their inherent sense of courage.

Lengthy suffering requires a great deal of courage, the kind of courage that cannot be taught, but rather is caught. This kind of courage is exemplified in Winston Churchill's 1940 "Finest Hour" speech before Parliament, uttered shortly before the Battle of Britain began. In that speech, Churchill galvanized all of Great Britain by offering only blood, toil, tears, and sweat. It was not forced measures he demanded, however, for it was his own courage that was on display.

9. Steere, *Spiritual Counsel and Letters of von Hügel*, 34.
10. Ibid., 4.

Sometimes sufferers display extraordinary courage—even joy—in the face of adversity. What is the explanation? In many cases it is the result of their spiritual condition, for courage belongs to the realm of the Spirit; as such, it comes from an inexhaustible supply. Like all things spiritual, the more we use it, the more we have. Doctor Tournier tells the story of one of his colleagues in medicine who for years had been treating a woman for anemia, without ever achieving a hemoglobin count of more than 68 percent. One day he found that it was over 80 percent. He asked her what had happened since her last visit, and she replied that she "had found faith." Because it is spiritual, courage comes from God. And when God calls us to make a courageous decision, God also gives the strength to bear the consequences.

Why is courage necessary in misfortune? Because in facing misfortune courageously we suffer far less than if we lapse into despair. Will power, however, is not enough. Behind courage is an attitude we call creativity. Behind all deprivation and suffering are opportunities for creativity. While it is not suffering that makes a person grow, one does not grow without suffering. While suffering may not be creative in itself, we are scarcely ever creative without suffering.

How is it that creativity results from deprivation? The answer comes from biological evolution, which teaches us that a succession of random errors in the duplication of the genetic code is the key to the evolution of living species. Marital conflict illustrates this process. Through a long series of small conflicts husbands and wives adapt to one another, producing a relationship that is more complex, productive, and solid than the simplistic relationship of a honeymoon. Those couples, however, who lack the courage to confront one another, who avoid conflict for the sake of peace, often become strangers to each other, allowing repressed grudges to erupt with catastrophic consequences.

How consoling it is to discover that we learn from our mistakes, and that we owe the wonderful diversity of living species to lapses in DNA—mistakes in copying the genetic code. How interesting that physics, the most scientific of disciplines, is the one to discover the discontinuous, random, and unforeseeable side of nature, of which all we can measure is its probability. This, then, is God's method, the art of using random mutations in order to accomplish the divine plan, akin to how God uses evil for our salvation. How comforting to know that God uses not only our strength but also our weakness to guide us.

The nutcracker illustrates our thesis perfectly. The shell of the nut represents the protective refuge that gradually becomes hardened by the routine of good health, vitality, and wellbeing. The shell encloses the tender fruit of creativity, newness, and change. Nutcrackers are those deprivations that disturb the ongoing process of life, fossilized in routine. The breaking of the nut is the calamity that strikes us. Which of us has not felt broken by some particular painful event? But there is another important side to this. The hard shell is the rigid, fixed framework of the genetic code, the habits, prejudices, and behavioral patterns that imprison us.[11]

The maxim, "history is but a succession of irremediable disasters," speaks of the cracking of the nut. Nevertheless, the nut cannot break open of itself. This, then, is our lesson, that what disturbs our lives, puts us out, irritates and makes us suffer, is what makes growth and development possible, on condition, of course, that we are not destroyed by it.

Think about what happens when calamity strikes. When something is broken in us, how do we respond? Generally by asking ourselves questions that tend to get forgotten in the routine of ordinary life—about the meaning of existence, suffering, pain, and death. Our materialistic world does not teach us how to cope with adversity, so we need to fall back on our creativity and imagination. Creativity has always been there, hidden, blocked by convention, but present within, the gift of God. The biblical writer expressed this aptly in Genesis 1:27: "So God created humankind in his image." Because God is Creator, to be in God's image is to be endowed with creativity. Hence our need for adventure, for newness and growth. Break the nut and you will discover the potential inside.

Questions for Discussion and Reflection

1. Have you ever viewed tragedy or illness as God's punishment for disobedience or sin? If you still believe this, why do you cling to this unchristian notion?

2. Do you believe God sends illness upon believers for their good or to accomplish divine ends? Why or why not?

3. In your estimation, can suffering or illness have a redemptive or vicarious purpose? Explain your answer.

---

11. Tournier, *Creative Suffering*, 129–31.

4. In your estimation, is it possible for God to suffer? If so, does God share in our suffering?

5. Have you ever felt closer to God in times of illness or personal tragedy? If so, describe your experience.

6. What contributions does the doctrine of the incarnation make to your experience and understanding of suffering?

7. What contributions does the doctrine of the resurrection make to your experience and understanding of suffering?

8. In your estimation, what did Friedrich von Hügel mean when he stated that there was "no joy without suffering?"

9. To those seeking greater depth in their spiritual journey, should this task be described with negative imagery—as a wilderness or desert, as darkness and emptiness—or with positive imagery—as an adventure or banquet, as splendor and fullness? Explain your answer.

CHAPTER 10

Experiencing God through Nature

Love all of God's creation, the whole and every grain in it.
Love every leaf, every ray of God's light.
Love the animals, love the plants, love everything.
If you love everything, you will perceive the divine mystery in things.

—Fyodor Dostoyevsky

As a young adult, one of my favorite books was *A Touch of Wonder*, by Arthur Gordon. The book was about commonplace events and everyday life, and how they were packed with joy, hope, love, and faith. Such qualities about which Gordon wrote with charm and grace seem enhanced when we engage fully with the natural world.

While most human beings enjoy the comfort and security of their homes, there is in all of us a love of nature, a desire to get outdoors on a pleasant day and experience the wonder and mystery of nature. Many people enjoy a walk in the park or through the woods, the exhilaration of a grand view after climbing a mountain. Others love camping and living outdoors wherever possible. Some people spend summers or weekends in natural settings, in the woods, by a lake, or near a beach. Why is this so? Because nature is our true home. Our ancestors lived in caves and tents, finding ways to survive. While life was tough, they lived in awe and wonder at nature, at its beauty, bounty, ferocity, and immensity. Nature was mysterious and marvelous.

"Two things fill the mind with ever-increasing wonder and awe," wrote the philosopher Immanuel Kant, "the starry heavens above and the moral law within." Albert Einstein said, "The most beautiful thing we can experience is the mysterious." Thomas Carlyle noted that wonder is the basis of worship.

There are essentially two types of human beings, those who think of life as an adventure and those who think of it as a problem. The first type is enthusiastic, energetic, resistant to shock, and responsive to challenge. The other is suspicious, hesitant, withholding, and self-centered. To the first group, life is hopeful and exciting. To the second, life is a potential ambush. If this analysis is correct, then the most valuable legacy we can pass on to the next generation is not money, property, or heirlooms, but a capacity for wonder and gratitude, a sense of aliveness and joy.

In his book, Gordon recalls the day he rode in a caboose, the time he tried to skin an alligator, and the trophy table in the hall where he and his siblings were encouraged to exhibit things they had found—snake skins, seashells, arrowheads, flowers—anything unusual or beautiful. He tells the story of a seven-year-old-boy roused from bed one summer night in a seaside cottage.

> Dazed with sleep, he heard his mother murmur about the lateness of the hour, heard his father laugh. Then he was borne in his father's arms, with the swiftness of a dream, down the porch steps, out onto the beach.
>
> Overhead the sky blazed with stars. "Watch!" his father said. And incredibly, as he spoke, one of the stars moved. In a streak of golden fire, it flashed across the astonished heavens. And before the wonder of this could fade, another star leaped from its place, and then another, plunging toward the restless sea. "What is it?" the child whispered. "Shooting stars," his father said. "They come every year on certain nights in August. I thought you'd like to see the show."[1]
>
> That was all: just an unexpected glimpse of something haunting and mysterious and beautiful. Back in bed, the child stared for a long time into the dark, rapt with the knowledge that all around the quiet house the night was full of the silent music of the falling stars.

Gordon admits he was that fortunate boy whose father believed that a new experience was more important for a child than an unbroken night's sleep. That moment was so great that it altered his childhood. He was never quite the same again.

Undoubtedly, each of us has a memorable story from nature: watching an eagle fly; experiencing a storm; swimming in the ocean or in a cold, mountain stream; watching a spectacular sunset. Many of my most

---

1. Gordon, *Touch of Wonder*, 167.

memorable experiences occurred while I pedaled a bicycle, whether as a youngster cycling from San José, the capital of Costa Rica, to the remote farm high in the mountains in San José de la Montaña, where I was raised, or in midlife cycling solo across the continental United States and in the Swiss Alps, Turkey, Israel, and Egypt.[2] When we experience nature this way, we feel fully alive. For those who can observe it, the divine shines through the living world. As Loren Eisley writes profoundly, the unfolding, growing, instinctive nature of birds and animals often reveals a purpose that points to the divine. Our natural sense of wonder opens us to astonishment and surprise, to the dimension of life we call spiritual.

Wonder, like playfulness, is a quality found in nearly all children. A thirst for learning emerges out of wonder. Perhaps the reason Jesus encouraged his followers to become as little children in order to enter the kingdom of God (that is, to experience God) is that children possess this sense of wonder and openness. The world for children has a magical quality, is enchanted.

Hinduism, perhaps the oldest and most complex of the world religions, maintains a view of reality described as monistic, meaning that all reality is ultimately one. According to this view, the cosmos is spiritual. Ultimately all things come from and return to the world soul (Brahma or brahman). The many deities of Hinduism are said to be temporal aspects of the world soul, which is eternal.

In Hindu mythology, the world is created by the self-sacrifice of God—"sacrifice" in its original sense means "to make sacred." So God becomes the world, which in the end becomes God again. The unfolding universe, viewed as the creative activity of the divine, is called *lila*, the play of God. Viewed thus, the cosmos and history are the stage of divine play.

This idea of life—whether human and nonhuman—as divine led Alan Watts, the author who interpreted Eastern philosophy to Western audiences, to speak of sin as the adult, unplayful action of taking oneself too seriously. Adults sin when they kill the child within. According to Watts, it is the pride of neglecting the child within—of failing to appreciate the playfulness of God—that "brought tragedy into the universe, marred the happiness that God created us to share, and made necessary redemption through the cross."[3] Watts speaks of children being happiest

---

2. These accounts are narrated in Vande Kappelle, *The Invisible Mountain* and *Into Thin Places*.

3. Watts, *Behold the Spirit*, 176.

when they simply take life as it comes, playing with pets, walking through fields, and taking risks. He find the same to be true of music: at its highest and best, music is pure play. "Playfulness, he concludes, is the very nature of divine wisdom."[4]

Have Christians misunderstood the doctrine of creation, grounded in the biblical Garden of Eden, an idyllic setting designed to foster the divine-human relationship? Have modern Christians so emphasized the story's mythological nature that they have neglected an essential aspect of the story, the fact that humans were created to enjoy intimacy with God through nature? According to the Genesis account, God walked "in the garden at the time of the evening breeze" (Gen. 3:8), seeking companionship with the humans he had made "in his image," that is, capable of relating with God. And how did Adam and Eve respond? They "hid themselves from the presence of the Lord God among the trees of the garden." Humans have been doing that ever since, using nature as an end rather than as a means for fellowship with God, using nature for recreation alone, rather than for re-creation.

"The heavens are telling the glory of God," says the psalmist, "and the firmament proclaims his handiwork" (Ps. 19:1). From its inception, the Christian tradition has viewed nature (creation) as a means of revelation. The concept of Two Books, the Book of Nature and the Book of Scripture, was first articulated by Tertullian (c. 160–c. 230), an early Christian theologian. Nature and scripture proceed alike from the creative Word of God, and, when properly interpreted, reveal truth that is not contradictory.

Francis of Assisi (1181–1226), founder of the Franciscan Order, had a great love for everything God had made. He is well known for preaching to the birds, but he loved everything in nature that was beautiful as belonging to God. Moreover, he saw everything natural as symbolic of God—sheep and lambs, surely, but also trees, rocks, and light. His *Canticle to the Sun*, written late in life, shows his love of the natural world. Bonaventure (1217–1274), known for writing deeply mystical works, joined the Franciscans in 1243 and took Francis's practical life orientation to the level of theology. He wrote, "unless we are able to view things in terms of . . . how God shines forth in them, we will not be able to understand."

Unlike most theologians of his time, Bonaventure paid little attention to sin, merit, justification, or atonement. His vision was mystical, cosmic, and intimately relational. He focused attention on perception and intuition,

---

4. Ibid., 179.

believing that a positive theology resulted in the enjoyment of life. Bonaventure's theology was not about fearing or placating a distant or angry God, but about delighting in God's all-pervasive plan. For Bonaventure, God is not an offended monarch throwing down mighty thunderbolts, but a fountain of fullness that flows and fills all things to overflowing.

Bonaventure's positive, coherent, and meaning-filled view of reality is at odds with the reward/punishment view that predominates when people merely uphold dogmatic propositions without experiencing God's presence. If modern Christians were able to recover Bonaventure's perspective of life, nature, and God, it could provide the framework society lacks in our age of cynicism and despair. In *The Soul's Journey into God*, Bonaventure expressed the Franciscan awareness of the presence of God in nature. Bonaventure envisioned nature in terms of cosmic connectedness. Quite simply, nature (creation), like Christ, is the mirror and image of the holy, God's "fingerprint" and "footprint." The physical universe, like the human soul, reflects God; each is a rung in the ladder leading to God. Theologians in this tradition give us confidence to believe that "everything belongs" in the circle of life. From this perspective, God "is the intelligible sphere whose center is everywhere and whose circumference is nowhere."

Having lived as a child on a two-hundred-acre farm high in the mountains of Costa Rica, the small country in Central America known for its rugged beauty, I always loved nature. The farm, home to eighty orphan children, was also a working coffee plantation. While my mother attended to the needs of the children, my father supervised the workers responsible for the farm's maintenance.

My father, a profoundly pietistic man who spent hours daily in prayer and Bible study, particularly in his retirement years, loved nature, and he spent as much time as possible outdoors, hiking, gardening, tending livestock, but always observing and pondering. In another life, he might have been a botanist or a zoologist, for he could identify every tree, flower, and bush by name. Despite his fascination and curiosity about the natural world, nature was never an end in itself, but a means to commune with God. If my father were alive today, he might be called a "nature mystic"; not one, however, who communes with nature for its own sake, but rather as one who views nature sacramentally. Nature, for him, was God's creation, and the goal was never nature but always nature's God.

According to John Haught, longtime professor of theology at Georgetown University and a leading contributor to the science and religion dialogue, when religion is wholesome it maintains four components: sacramental, mystical, silent, and active. Each of these dimensions suggests a distinct "way" of being religious, he argues, "but religion is most healthy and alive when it blends all four ways harmoniously. And it begins to dissolve into something other than 'religion' whenever any of the four aspects is isolated from contact with its three partners. In the actual world of religious life, such sundering of one aspect from the others is not unusual. But when this splintering occurs, religion rapidly decays into magic, escapism, or obsession with esoteric teachings, or into cynicism, iconoclasm, or vacuous activism."[5] When, on the other hand, religion concretely preserves the four components in a balanced way, it functions in an ecologically supportive way.

Of these, I am fascinated by the sacramental dimension. Religion is sacramental in the sense that it can speak of unspeakable mystery only through the use of symbols, or what theology calls sacraments. A sacrament, in its broadest sense, includes any object, person or event through which religious consciousness is awakened to the presence of sacred mystery. Historically, most of religion's sacraments have been closely related to nature. For example, the luminosity of sunshine, dawn, and dusk; the experience of wind or breath; the purifying power of clean water; the fertility of soil and life—all of these natural phenomena, and many more, have been used by religions to symbolize the way in which ultimate mystery affects us.

Since nature provides many of the fundamental sacraments of human religion, it is easy to see how the conservation of nature is indispensable for the survival of religion. If we lose the environment, we lose God as well. And it is equally true that when religion loses touch with its sacramental origins, it begins to grow indifferent to the natural world. A sacramental vision, Haught reminds us, makes nature transparent to divinity. In this sense it concedes to nature an inherent value without allowing it to become a substitute for God. According to this Christian perspective, nature is worth saving not because it is sacred, but because it is sacramental.

Because nature, properly understood, mediates the sacred, the writer Fyodor Dostoyevsky once exhorted his reader, "Love all of God's creation, the whole and every grain of sand in it. Love every leaf, every ray of God's light. Love the animals, love the plants, love everything. If you love everything, you will perceive the divine mystery in things."

In his book *Prayer*, Richard Foster tells an interesting story:

5. Haught, *Promise of Nature*, 73–75.

Once I was leading a worship service in a home on a hot summer evening. The doors were left open in hopes of a breeze. At one point in the meeting I encouraged everyone to "wait on the Lord" in listening silence. The stillness, however, was quickly interrupted by the homeowner's cat scratching at the screen door, seeking entrance. The more I tried to ignore the cat, the worse it got. I prayed that God would do something—send the cat away, magically open the door, and other more drastic prayers that I shall not mention, since you may have a fondness for cats. (Strangely, it never occurred to me to get up and let the cat in!)

Later in the evening someone mentioned the cat. Everyone began sharing how distracting the cat had been to their ability to focus on God. Everyone, that is, except Bill—a former missionary filled with wisdom and the Holy Spirit. Bill sat pensive, uttering not a word. "Bill," I queried, "what are you thinking?" "Oh," he spoke deliberately, "I was just wondering what God wanted to say to us through the cat" . . . I was looking upon the cat as a distraction; Bill was looking upon the cat as a possible messenger. And that may well be enough "message" for anyone for one evening.[6]

If, according to Einstein, "science without religion is lame, and religion without science is blind," then surely religion without wonder is dead. Is wonder dead today? Not necessarily, but I believe it has been transformed into curiosity, something that can be satisfied more by searching the Web than by going outdoors. According to New Testament scholar Dale Allison, human migration from the country to the city—a process that has occurred relentlessly in the past century—has alienated religion from nature, for the more humans have moved indoors, the less inclined they have become to believe. In the past, Allison writes, the stars above nurtured human wonder as much as anything else. Traditional mythologies, poetry, fiction—all are filled with stories about the heavenly bodies. The reason is simple: in the past people spent time outdoors, sleeping under the heavenly canopy. The sky and its lights dazzled and mystified. They evoked stories and thoughts of realities beyond human grasp, both visible and invisible.

Today most people are asleep when the sun rises and inside when it sets. When people do venture outdoors at night, artificial light blunts their vision and their curiosity. As the stars fade from our direct experience, Allison laments, our hearts are made different from the hearts of our predecessors. As a result, we have lost our best illustration of the concept of transcendence, for

---

6. Foster, *Prayer*, 86.

the stars represent "the one constant reminder that there are things of whose existence we may know but whose nature ever escapes our knowledge."[7]

The essence of light, physicists tell us, is unknown. Sometimes it appears as a particle, sometimes as a wave. Photons, we are told, have neither mass nor charge. If light is not reflected or refracted, it altogether disappears, as though nonexistent. The analogy with God is remarkable. As Annie Dillard suggests, apart from nature, God disappears. If we are to relate to God, we should use "any means ready at hand."[8] The Book of Nature—ever at hand—is a resource we cannot ignore if we are to practice the presence of God.

Questions for Discussion and Reflection

1. Do you tend to view the glass as half-empty or as half-full? In other words, is the natural world more like a garden or a briar patch?
2. What memories of nature do you have from your childhood? Did you view nature through the eyes of wonder or through the eyes of fear? Explain your answer.
3. As an adult, have you retained your sense of playfulness? If so, why? If not, why not?
4. How can we move from viewing nature as recreational to viewing nature as re-creational?
5. Some modern theologians disagree with the concept of Two Books, viewing nature as sinful and fallen and therefore as an unreliable means of revelation, Others, like Francis of Assisi and Bonaventure, believe that nature, properly interpreted, reveals God and truth as reliably as scripture. On which side of the debate do you stand? Explain your answer.
6. Describe the value of viewing nature sacramentally.
7. In your estimation, can God speak to humans through animals? Explain your answer.
8. Do you agree with New Testament scholar Dale Allison that as humans have moved indoors, they are less inclined to believe? Explain your answer.

7. Allison, *Luminous Dusk*, 8.
8. Dillard, *Holy the Firm*, 55.

EPILOGUE

The Kingdom of Heaven

The kingdom of God is not coming with things that can be observed....
in fact, the kingdom of God is within you.

—Luke 17:20–21

My love affair with scripture began at the age of four, lasted through a forty-year teaching career in the field of biblical studies, and has not wavered since. For two thousand years the Bible, in part or in whole, has been viewed as sacred by generations of believers, its sacredness related not to the origin of the Bible but rather to its status within the Christian community. For Christians, the status of the Bible as sacred scripture means it is the primary collection of writings they know, definitive for faith and practice. The sacredness of scripture is validated by its ability to inspire believers in every age, thereby authenticating its enduring message. Of all the world's religions and scriptures, the Christian Bible presents the best picture of God, of the spiritual nature of human beings, and of the spiritual world that surrounds us.

At the heart of the Bible stands an individual, Jesus of Nazareth, to whom the Old Testament scriptures point, and on whose life and teaching the New Testament scriptures build. And the dominant theme in the preaching of Jesus—indeed the center of his mission and message—is the coming of the kingdom of God. While the phrase "kingdom of God" is rare in contemporary Jewish writings, it is widely regarded as one of the most distinctive aspects of the preaching of Jesus. Because almost everywhere in the Old Testament the idea of the kingdom is related to the people of Israel and the rule of the house of David in Jerusalem, Jesus is at pains to divest his teaching of this former understanding of the nature of the kingdom.

What did Jesus mean when he spoke of the kingdom? We touched on this subject in chapter 6, noting that Jesus' views about God and God's kingdom were central to his teaching, constituting unique points of emphasis in his ministry. The term "kingdom" is complex and paradoxical at its core. In the Synoptic Gospels, the paradoxical nature of the kingdom is manifested in several ways: (a) it is present (Matt. 12:28; Luke 17:21), yet not fully present (Matt. 8:29; 13:30); (b) it is a gift (Matt. 25:34; Luke 12:32), yet it also involves human effort (Matt. 6:33; Luke 12:31); (c) it is an internal reality (Luke 17:20–21), yet it has external implications for the world (Matt. 6:10). Scholars are particularly interested in the first of these, for it addresses the tension between the present time and the future, the "already" and the "not yet." In that regard, they have introduced the term "inaugurated eschatology" to refer to the relation of the present inauguration and the future fulfillment of the kingdom.

There is a present element in the New Testament concept of the kingdom, particularly in the teaching of Jesus, which is colored by a sense of intense urgency. God has already taken the initiative; humans are challenged to recognize the reality of the present situation and to make such decisions as will qualify them to become citizens of the kingdom. The signs of the presence of the kingdom are already present in the ministry of Jesus. When John the Baptist questions the mission of Jesus and asks for signs, he is given clear evidence: "the blind receive their sight, the lame walk, the lepers are cleansed, the deaf hear, the dead are raised, and the poor have good news brought to them" (Matt. 11:5). All these are signs that the power of the kingdom is presently at work. Those who refuse to recognize that the power evident in Jesus is a power from God are told: "if it is by the finger of God that I cast out the demons, then the kingdom of God has come to you" (Luke 11:20). When one person, for a period of some thirty-five years, lives in total dependence upon God, with a unique understanding of God's will and in unconditional surrender to it, the kingdom is already present. As Jesus tells the Pharisees in answer to their question about when the kingdom was coming: "the kingdom of God is within you" (Luke 17:21).

According to the New Testament, Christians are kind of hybrid creatures who live in two dimensions. They are citizens of the present age while at the same time living under the dominion of Christ's kingdom. As Paul put it somewhat paradoxically, Christians live "in the flesh" (human nature) and also "in the Spirit" (the new dimension introduced by Christ). Awareness of this dual citizenship led early Christians to say that they were "strangers" in the historical era on earth (Heb. 11:13).

Ever since the New Testament period Christianity has had to steer between two dangers. On the one hand, Christians have been tempted to

EPILOGUE: THE KINGDOM OF HEAVEN

withdraw from society on the assumption that Christ's kingdom is not of this world (John 18:36). On the other hand, they have been tempted to make a too easy identification of the kingdom with something in this world, such as the institutional church or the ideal human society. However, the essential message of the New Testament is this: The kingdom is not of this world, yet it has been manifest in this world through the life, death, and resurrection of Christ. Although God's kingdom is a higher order than any political reality or human ideal of the present age, it has influenced and penetrated the kingdoms of this world—not as a tangent touches a circle but as a vertical line intersects a horizontal plane. The task of the church is to bear witness to this "vertical dimension" of history and, in so doing, to seek to leaven and redeem society in the name of Christ. This attitude toward society is not one of "detachment" but one of "transfiguration," involving a rhythm of withdrawal and return through worship and action, faith and good works.

For those interested in understanding how Jesus' teachings on the kingdom affect faith and practice, a good place to begin is the Sermon on the Mount, found in Matthew 5–7 (an abbreviated and revised version appears in Luke's Sermon on the Plain; 6:17-49). This so-called "sermon" should not be considered as having been delivered by Jesus on one occasion, but was most likely formed by the author of Matthew's Gospel for his community, gathered from collections of memorized sayings of Jesus. Some find here a new moral code, to be followed literally, while others, noting the severity of the standards, call them "interim ethics," supposing that Jesus' envisioned them as rules applicable only in a time of crisis.[1]

At the heart of the Sermon on the Mount we find these words: "But strive first for the kingdom of God and his righteousness" (Matt. 6:33). According to this teaching, the kingdom is to be the believer's first and main concern. It was certainly so for Jesus, who gave up everything for the sake of the kingdom.

Finding myself among the many biblical scholars fascinated by Jesus' teaching on the kingdom, I too have been attracted to this concept, in part because of its enigmatic nature. While doing research for this book, I came across Morton Kelsey's book *Afterlife*, and found in it a unique understanding of the kingdom, one I had never heard before. According to Kelsey, "the

---

1. Albert Schweitzer coined the phrase "interim ethics" to express his belief that Jesus understood himself to be living at the end of human history. The interim period was to be short; hence the stern ethic.

central message of Jesus of Nazareth is about heaven."[2] With that statement, Kelsey indicates that when Jesus used the phrase "kingdom of God," he was speaking about heaven directly rather than indirectly about God's presence or God's rule.[3]

My initial reaction upon reading Kelsey's statement was perplexity, for it sounded like something I had heard repeatedly through the course of my life and had rejected, namely, that the main concern of Christians on earth should be about how to get to heaven. But that is not what Kelsey meant. As he states, when Jesus spoke about heaven, those who heard him were amazed, because Jesus' message differed "in two ways from anything they had heard before. They knew about hoping for heaven in the future and trying their best to earn it and avoid punishment. But Jesus spoke about finding heaven within and around and among us, as well as in a future hidden from us. Heaven, he said, is at hand. . . . Heaven, Jesus taught, can be shared in the here and now. It is both the immediate goal toward which we work in this life, and also the gift we hope to be given in the end."[4] What Mark and Luke call "the kingdom of God," what Matthew calls the "kingdom of heaven," and what John calls "eternal life," is a reality both present now and hereafter, both immanent and transcendent.

According to Kelsey, the key to understanding the nature of the kingdom, that is, the key to understanding what heaven is like, is given at the start of the Sermon on the Mount. Because Jesus spoke of the kingdom (heaven) repeatedly, using a variety of images to speak of the concept, the best place to go for a comprehensive view, for a blueprint or working plan of the kingdom, is the eight Beatitudes found in Matthew 5:3–12.

Whether this passage is directly from the mouth of Jesus or a summary by those well acquainted with his teaching makes little difference. Either way, it summarizes Jesus' teaching about the kingdom, highlighting the qualities that characterize those who experience God in the present and in the afterlife. The blessed, or fortunate, are those who encounter God in life and therefore find ultimate meaning.

---

2. Kelsey, *Afterlife*, 157.

3. As is commonly known, the Gospel of Matthew often substitutes the expression "kingdom of heaven," for "kingdom of God," using "heaven" as a circumlocution for "God." The usual explanation for this peculiarity is that Matthew was writing primarily to a Jewish audience, which preferred to address God or to speak about God indirectly rather than directly, using terms such as "The Name" or "heaven" as substitutes for "God" or for "deity."

4. Kelsey, *Afterlife*, 157–58.

EPILOGUE: THE KINGDOM OF HEAVEN

A reading of the Beatitudes indicates that the result or reward is the same in the first and in the last Beatitude ("for theirs is the kingdom of heaven," Matt. 5:3, 10). These identical promises enclose the six intervening statements like parentheses. It seems reasonable, then, to take all eight statements as descriptions of God's kingdom, the kingdom of heaven. What Jesus tells us in this passage, then, is two things: the nature of heaven, and the fact that we can participate initially in its reality now and more fully after death.

Keys to the Kingdom of Heaven[5]

The eight qualities found in the Beatitudes—the poor in spirit, those who mourn, the meek, those who hunger and thirst for righteousness, the merciful, the pure in heart, the peacemakers, and those who are persecuted for righteousness' sake—are not steps that individuals must take consecutively to reach the fortunate or blessed state, but are more like keys to doors, "any one of which will swing open and let a person enter the kingdom of heaven."[6]

Entrance into the kingdom is not what we ordinarily think. The world of Jesus Christ, of heavenly spirituality, is unlike ordinary human standards. As Jesus saw it, we do not enter the kingdom because we are wise or powerful or intelligent, but rather because we are childlike and seeking, aware that all is not well. In the kingdom, the first are last and the last first. If it is the dispossessed and unfortunate, the gentle and merciful, who become citizens of the kingdom, how then can ordinary individuals prepare for the world we call heaven, where God dwells? The descriptions that Jesus gave in the Beatitudes point the way. Here we find the kind of attitudes and actions that will enable us to experience the kingdom here and now. And these are the attitudes and actions that will allow us to share fully in that same kingdom after death.

Each of us has his or her redeeming quality. According to Carl Jung's depiction of personality types, the sensing person has the virtue of simplicity, the intuitive person of wisdom, the thinking type of justice, and the feeling person of joy. In addition, each person has a unique way of entering the kingdom, and each must find the doorway that represents entrance.

---

5. This segment is adapted from Kelsey, *Afterlife*, 186–211.
6. Ibid., 187.

Let us examine the eight keys to the kingdom that Jesus describes in the Beatitudes and see what pattern of life they suggest.

- *The poor in spirit.* This quality, while it includes those who are materially poor, refers primarily to those who are inwardly poor, that is, those whose spirits are not inflated and arrogant. Because they are often detached from worldly attachments, the poor in spirit are open to new dimensions of reality. They are aware of inner conflict and realize that they cannot cope without saving help. The teachings of Jesus repeatedly stress that the surest way to gain one's life or one's self-esteem is to lose it, while those who continue to put their own pride and self-conceit first will end up losers. What this means for us today is that our most valiant efforts to hold the right beliefs and to do the right thing will fail if they result in self-satisfaction and arrogance. The moment we think we can earn God's favor, the door to spiritual development begins to close. Only those who can accept the kingdom as a gift, unearned and unmerited, are able to enter.

- *Those who mourn.* Many events make us feel the emotion of sorrow; the most common is bereavement, the loss of someone we love. However, one may also grieve loss of security, honor, or position. Others mourn because there is so much suffering in the world, and they feel helpless to make a difference. Jesus often speaks of repentance; he asked people first to confront themselves, and then to react with regret and sorrow. The sorrowful are those who mourn over their inner and outer poverty and allow repentance to permeate their whole being. As it does, something happens to them, and a new kind of life begins to emerge. Grief is cured only as we pass through it, not through avoidance. Bearing sorrow and grief enlarges one's heart. Only those who pass through sorrow and mourning can help others face similar problems.

- *The meek.* The gentle or the meek include the poor in spirit and those who mourn. Such people are not puffed up with pride or arrogance but are humble, considerate, and unassuming. They treat others as equals, and they work to create conditions that allow others to develop more fully their capacities. The meek are resourceful and hopeful, facilitators who do not force their own goals onto others but rather accept others as they are. Gentleness, however, is not weakness, This quality of life is more like the resilience of a reed growing by a stream.

The reed bends with the wind and survives. Even a gale cannot uproot it, while the mighty oak may be torn from its roots and left to die.

- *Those who hunger and thirst for righteousness.* "Hunger" and "thirst" speak of the human desire to seek fulfillment of the deep searching of the human heart. To hunger and thirst means to desire something strongly. In kingdom language, these terms refer to one's love for God. In John's account of the feeding of the five thousand, Jesus spoke of bread from heaven and told the people, "I am the bread of life. Whoever comes to me will never be hungry, and whoever believes in me will never be thirsty" (John 6:35). In the New Testament, righteousness is more than simply moral and legal aspects of right thinking and action. Paul suggests that people do not become righteous simply by following the law, but rather by accepting God's grace humbly. According to scripture, one becomes righteous when one hungers and thirsts for fellowship with God.

- *The merciful.* Most of us find it difficult to be merciful, for mercy involves forgiveness, and it is not easy to forgive those who hurt us. Jesus was clear about the importance of mercy and forgiveness. In the Lord's Prayer he included only one condition: we can expect God to give freely all that we need, including forgiveness, so long as we are able to forgive others. Charles Williams wrote in his book *The Forgiveness of Sins* that there are things that need not be forgiven, things that ought to be forgiven, and things that cannot be forgiven—and that the Christian is to forgive them all. How do we achieve this quality of life? Mercy flows naturally from a life marked by meekness and poverty of spirit.

- *The pure in heart.* We have a tendency to think of the heart in medical terms, as an organ that pumps blood through the body. The Greek language, however, views the heart as the center and source of inner life. It gives rise to all that makes us human. To be "pure" is to be sincere and single-minded. In his book *Purity of Heart*, the Danish philosopher Søren Kierkegaard suggested that purity of heart means to be directed toward one goal, to be motivated by one central passion. Within each of us are many different powers and voices, different desires competing for control. Our task, as followers of Christ, is to bring this motley crew together into one, undivided personality. This cannot happen unless we realize our poverty of spirit and pray to have all parts of our being brought together into harmony by an act of God's grace. In his teaching, Jesus warned that no one can serve two masters (Matt. 6:22–24), and that every kingdom divided against itself cannot stand (Matt. 12:25). Purity of heart, like poverty of spirit and righteousness, is a gift given to those who realize they are unable to satisfy the hunger and thirst of their souls. Purity of heart, however, is more than an attitude, a condition, or a state of life. It is the willingness to know oneself and to bring every aspect of one's life into harmonious relation with the kingdom and its goals.

- *The peacemakers.* In the Lord's Prayer we ask for God's will to be done and for God's kingdom to come on earth as it is in heaven. Peacemakers are committed to this goal. They work not only to bring harmony and peace to those around them but also to experience harmony and health within. Those who taste God's love come to know the peace—the harmony and blessed joy—that is an essential quality of God's kingdom. Such people are called children of God. As peacemakers, they share in the nature of God. Growing in peace within, they also work to bring peace to others.

- *Those who are persecuted for righteousness' sake.* Jesus warned his followers that discipleship might lead to opposition and persecution. While society has changed since the first century, particularly in the West, where Christianity is the norm, the world still has ways of showing contempt for those who desire more than conventional religion. While such suffering can open a door into God's kingdom, this does not mean that we can find that doorway by inviting persecution or martyrdom. The church condemns all forms of violence and self-destructiveness, even that of martyrdom. The way of the kingdom, the way of the cross, requires courage as well as meekness. Meekness without courage can become weakness and sentimentality. Those who cannot enter the kingdom by way of peacemaking, humility, or mourning can enter through the door of courage, steadfastness, and forbearance.

The Blessings of the Kingdom of Heaven[7]

As with the eight qualities of the kingdom, the six results[8] describe blessings both present and future, the results found among those who are

---

7. This segment is adapted from Kelsey, *Afterlife*, 168–185.
8. As noted above, two of the eight results or rewards are identical ("for theirs is the

EPILOGUE: THE KINGDOM OF HEAVEN

able to live in contact with God as the source of ultimate meaning. In the Beatitudes Jesus is giving us his picture of God's kingdom, for whose coming we are to pray daily (Matt. 6:10). What, then, are the blessings available to those who make God's kingdom, that is, relationship with God, a priority? These six qualities represent the best picture of heaven, of God's kingdom, ever given:

- *They will be comforted*, that is, they will be healed of all sorrow and anguish. The Greek word "to comfort or console" is the word from which "paraclete" or "comforter" is taken, a reference in John's Gospel to the Holy Spirit. The person who is comforted is not just soothed and relieved of misery, but is strengthened, reconstituted, and re-established. Those who are comforted begin to see life more from God's perspective, from an eternal stance; it is the state of reality in which the victory of Jesus' resurrection is reaffirmed and realized.

- *They will inherit the earth*, that is, they will be committed to improving the state of things here on earth. As heirs, they will work with God to provide the care God's earth needs.

- *They will be filled*, that is, they will experience wholeness and wellbeing. The word in Greek for "being filled" comes from the word for hay and was used to describe cattle being filled and satisfied. If you have ever seen a cow eat, you will note that a cow gets filled slowly and gradually. To be filled, we must acquire patience: too much too fast may well choke us. As Augustine put it, God made us for himself, and we cannot know rest or satisfaction until we find it in God. The best pictures of the kingdom—of heaven—suggest that we shall be slowly transformed through eternity, until we become the kind of people we have always wanted to be. Then we shall find visions of new potentials and gradually move toward new goals, each filling more complete than the last.

- *They will receive mercy*, that is, they will experience unconditional forgiveness. God is not just, but merciful. Heaven—the kingdom—is not a place of retribution, but a place of forgiveness, mercy, and love. Only as we experience love and forgiveness in our ordinary lives do we begin to understand that this is what God and God's eternal kingdom are like. Hell, as someone has said, can be described as a state of

---

kingdom of heaven"), leaving six distinct results.

eternal obsession with guilt, so that one is unable to accept forgiveness. The unique idea of Christianity is that humans do not need to suffer from guilt and self-condemnation. Heaven is the state of being in which we are given a fresh start.

- *They will see God*, that is, they will experience the Beloved. Here on earth we must be content with experiencing the presence of God; in eternity we shall come "face to face with the Love that lights our inner being."[9] When we come to the center, finding there the source of all things, we will know that we are accepted, loved, desired.

- *They will be called children of God*, that is, they will accept their service in life like the pure play of children, full of joy, fun, and excitement. The children of God are also God's co-workers, and this is what makes them inheritors of earth. Each image speaks of a different aspect of the same truth. Children, sons and daughters, not only rest with their parents, they also work and play with them. In a similar way, in heaven we can expect joy and fulfillment as well as participation in all of God's activity.

Paul, in speaking about heaven, can only grasp at straws when he says, "No eye has seen, nor ear heard, nor the human heart conceived, what God has prepared for those who love him" (1 Cor. 2:9). Neither an eternal life that is already fully achieved here below, nor an eternal life begun and known solely in the beyond, satisfies our deepest spiritual longing. Only an eternal life already begun and truly known in part here, though fully achieved and completely understood hereafter, corresponds to the deepest longing of our human spirit as touched by God. May that, dear reader, be your experience, now and forever.

If we understand the kingdom correctly, God, it seems, appears far more interested in communicating with us than we are in communicating with God. God has taken the initiative by creating a spiritually rich universe, one that provides multiple pathways for contact, relationship, and even intimacy. The ball is in your court. How will you respond?

---

9. Ibid, 179.

EPILOGUE: THE KINGDOM OF HEAVEN

Questions for Discussion and Reflection

1. What does it mean historically when Christians affirm the sacredness of scripture? Would you characterize the Bible's role in this way, or is there a better term, image, or phrase you would use concerning the Bible's role in your life? Explain your answer.

2. How do you understand Jesus, as human, divine, incarnated Lord, resurrected Christ, or none of the above? Explain your answer.

3. What did Jesus mean when he spoke of the kingdom of God? What is your understanding of this concept? What synonym would you use to describe God's kingdom?

4. In your estimation, how was the kingdom of God evident in the life, death, and resurrection of Jesus?

5. What is your current understanding of "heaven"? Do you find it better to speak of heaven as a present reality on earth, as both a present (earthly) and future (eternal) reality, or as only a future reality? Explain your answer.

6. With which of the Beatitudes do you most relate? Which one seems most attractive? Explain your answer.

7. *For personal reflection*: Having finished this study, what have you learned? (Try stating your answer in one sentence.) How is God present in your life? How is asking you to respond to that presence?

Bibliography

Allison, Dale C., Jr. *The Luminous Dusk: Finding God in the Deep, Still Places.* Grand Rapids, MI: Eerdmans, 2006.
Bass, Diana Butler. *Christianity After Religion.* New York: HarperOne, 2012.
Bornkamm, Günther. *Jesus of Nazareth.* New York: Harper & Brothers, 1960.
Brueggemann, Walter. *Theology of the Old Testament.* Minneapolis: Fortress, 1997.
Buber, Martin. *I and Thou.* 2nd ed. New York: Scribners, 1958.
Buechner, Frederick. *Listening to Your Life.* New York: HarperOne, 1992.
Cullmann, Oscar. *Christ and Time.* Philadelphia: Westminster, 1950.
Dawkins, Richard. *The God Delusion.* New York: Houghton Mifflin, 2006.
Dillard, Annie. *Holy the Firm.* New York: Harper Colophon, 1977.
———. *Pilgrim at Tinker Creek.* New York: Bantam, 1974.
Eliade, Mircea. *Shamanism: Archaic Techniques of Ecstasy.* Princeton, NJ: Princeton University Press, 1970.
Foster, Richard J. *Celebration of Discipline: The Path to Spiritual Growth.* Rev. ed. New York: HarperSanFrancisco, 1998.
———. *Prayer: Finding the Heart's True Home.* New York: HarperSanFrancisco, 1992.
———. *Study Guide for Celebration of Discipline.* New York: Harper & Row, 1983.
Foster, Richard J., and James Bryan Smith. *Devotional Classics.* Rev. ed. New York: HarperOne, 2005.
Fox, Matthew. *The Coming of the Cosmic Christ.* New York: HarperSanFrancisco, 1988.
———. *Original Blessing: A Primer in Creation Spirituality.* Santa Fe, NM: Bear & Company, 1983.
Freud, Sigmund. *The Future of an Illusion.* New York; Doubleday, 1964.
Gordon, Arthur. *A Touch of Wonder.* New York: Fleming H. Revell, 1974.
Greeley, Andrew. *The Sociology of the Paranormal: A Reconnaissance.* Beverley Hills, CA: Sage, 1975.
Hall, Thelma. *Too Deep for Words: Rediscovering Lectio Divina.* New York: Paulist, 1988.
Haught, John F. *The Promise of Nature.* New York: Paulist, 1993.
Heisenberg, Werner. *Physics and Philosophy: The Revolution in Modern Science.* New York: Harper & Row, 1958.
Hendry, George S. *Theology of Nature.* Philadelphia: Westminster, 1980.
Holmes, Urban. *A History of Christian Spirituality.* New York: Seabury, 1980.
Huxley, Aldous. *Doors of Perception.* New York: Harper & Row, 1970.
James, William. *The Varieties of Religious Experience.* New York: Routledge, 2008 (1902).
Jones, Alan. *Journey into Christ.* New York: Seabury, 1977.

———. *Soul Making: The Desert Way of Spirituality*. New York: HarperSanFrancisco, 1985.
Jung, Carl G. *Memories, Dreams, Reflections*. New York: Pantheon, 1963.
———. *Modern Man in Search of a Soul*. New York: Harcourt, Brace and World, Inc., 1933.
Kasper, Walter. *Jesus the Christ*. New York: Paulist, 1976.
Keating, Thomas. *Intimacy with God: An Introduction to Centering Prayer*. New York: Crossroad, 1994.
———. *Intimacy with God*. No pages. Online: www.norumbega,net>path>iwg.
———. *Open Mind, Open Heart*. New York: Continuum, 1986.
Kelsey, Morton T. *Afterlife: The Other Side of Dying*. New York: Crossroad, 2005.
———. *Companions on the Inner Way: The Art of Spiritual Guidance*. New York: Crossroad, 1983.
———. *Encounter with God: A Theology of Christian Experience*. Minneapolis: Bethany, 1972.
———. *The Other Side of Silence: A Guide to Christian Meditation*. New York: Paulist, 1976.
———. *Reaching: The Journey to Fulfillment*. San Francisco: Harper & Row, 1989.
Kübler-Ross, Elisabeth. *On Death and Dying*. New York, Macmillan, 1969.
Kuhn, T. S. *The Structure of Scientific Revolution*. 2nd ed. Chicago: University of Chicago Press, 1970.
Lamott, Anne. *Plan B: Further Thoughts on Faith*. New York: Riverhead, 2005.
Lawrence, Brother. *The Practice of the Presence of God*. Mount Vernon, NY: Peter Pauper, 1963.
Lewis, C. S. *The Problem of Pain*. New York: Macmillan, 1962.
Loftus, John W. *The Christian Delusion: Why Faith Fails*. Amherst, NY: Prometheus, 2010.
MacKenzie, Charles. "Kant's Copernican Revolution," in Hoffecker, Andrew and Gary Scott Smith, *Building a Christian World View*. Vol. 1. Phillipsburg, NJ: Presbyterian and Reformed, 1986.
May, Gerald G. *Care of Mind, Care of Spirit*. San Francisco; Harper& Row, 1982.
———. *The Dark Night of the Soul*. New York: HarperSanFrancisco, 2004.
McLoughlin, William. *Revivals, Awakenings, and Reform*. Chicago: University of Chicago Press, 1978.
Merton, Thomas. *New Seeds of Contemplation*. Boston: Shambhala, 2013.
Moore, Thomas. *Care of the Soul: A Guide for Cultivating Depth and Sacredness in Everyday Life*. New York: Harper Perennial, 1992.
Nouwen, Henri J. M. *Reaching Out: The Three Movements of the Spiritual Life*. New York; Image, 1975.
———. *The Wounded Healer: Ministry in Contemporary Society*. Garden City, NY: Image, 1979.
Otto, Rudolph. *The Idea of the Holy*. New York: Oxford University Press, 1950.
Packer, James I. *Knowing God*. Downers Grove, IL: InterVarsity, 1973.
Peck, M. Scott. *The Road Less Traveled*. New York: Simon & Schuster, 1979.
Perrin, Norman. *The Kingdom of God in the Teaching of Jesus*. Philadelphia: Westminster, 1963.
———. *Rediscovering the Teaching of Jesus*. New York: Harper & Row, 1967.
Rohr, Richard. *Falling Upward: A Spirituality for the Two Halves of Life*. San Francisco: Jossey-Bass, 2011.

BIBLIOGRAPHY

———. *The Universal Christ*. New York: Convergent, 2019.
Sanford, John A. *The Kingdom Within*. Rev. ed. New York: HarperSanFrancisco, 1987.
Slater, Philip. *Wealth Addiction*. New York: E. P. Dutton, 1980.
Sorenson, Amanda and Stephen. *My Time with God*. Nashville, TN: Thomas Nelson, 1991.
Steere, Douglas V. *Spiritual Counsel and Letters of Baron Friedrich von Hügel*. New York: Harper & Row, 1964.
Tart, Charles. *Altered States of Consciousness*. New York: John Wiley & Sons, Inc., 1969.
Vande Kappelle. Robert P. *Beyond Belief: Faith, Science, and the Value of Unknowing*. Eugene, OR: Wipf & Stock, 2012.
———. *Dark Splendor: Spiritual Fitness for the Second Half of Life*. Eugene, OR: Resource, 2015.
———. *Into Thin Places: One Man's Search for the Center*. Eugene, OR: Resource, 2011.
———. *The Invisible Mountain: A Journey of Faith*. Eugene, OR: Resource, 2010.
———. *Iron Sharpens Iron: A Discussion Guide for Twenty-First-Century Seekers*. Eugene, OR: Wipf & Stock, 2013.
Von Hügel, Friedrich. *The Mystical Element of Religion as Studied in Saint Catherine of Genoa and her Friends*. 2 vols. 2nd ed. New York: E. P. Dutton, 1923.
Watts, Alan. *Behold the Spirit: A Study in the Necessity of Mystical Religion*. New York: Pantheon, 1947.
Wickes, Frances. *The Inner World of Childhood*. Rev. ed. New York: Appleton Century, 1966.
Yancey, Philip. *Disappointment with God*. Grand Rapids, MI: Zondervan, 1988.
———. *Finding God in Unexpected Places*. New York: Doubleday, 2005.
———. *Prayer; Does It Make Any Difference?* Grand Rapids, MI: Zondervan, 2006.
———. *Where Is God When It Hurts?* Grand Rapids, MI: Zondervan, 1997.

Index

addiction, 56
adolescence, 23
adulthood, 23
afterlife, 13, 34–35, 57
    See also heaven
agnostic(ism), 7, 9, 10, 14, 15
Allison, Dale, 127
apophatic tradition, 33, 42, 43, 50, 82
Aquinas, Thomas, 12, 68
archetypes, 40
Aristotle, 12. 30
artistic inspiration, 20, 40
ascetic(ism), 45
atheist, atheism, 7–9, 10
    existentialist, 10, 15
    inadequacy of, 11–14
    varieties of, 14–16
Augustine of Hippo, 18, 29, 68, 137
awakenings. *See* revivals and awakenings

Bass, Diana Butler, 27
Beatitudes, 52, 133–38
behaviorism, 15
Berdyaev, Nikolai, 15
Berry, Wendell, 109
Bible, 97–99, 129
    four senses of, 102–5
Bible reading, 77, 83, 91, 97–105
Blake, William, 20, 33
Boehme, Jacob, 33
Bonaventure, 18, 124–25
Borg, Marcus, 97
Bornkamm, Günther, 63
Brother Lawrence, 2, 50–55, 109
Brueggemann, Walter, 66

Buber, Martin, 74, 80
Buechner, Frederick, 80, 91
Byron, Lord, 33

Calvin, John, 18
Camus, Albert, 10
Carlyle, Thomas, 121
Carmichael, Amy, 50
Castro, Fidel, 113
celibacy, 45
Centering Prayer, 88, 89, 90, 100, 101
Chardin, Pierre Teilhard de, 16
charismatic gifts, 2, 28, 37–38, 44
children, childhood, 19–20, 22–23, 24,
    25, 41, 96, 123, 123–24, 138
church, 38, 95–97
    as body of Christ, 38, 79
    attendance, 27, 81
    failure of, 11, 15, 28, 30
    functions of, 11
Churchill, Winston, 117
collective unconscious, 40
Comte, Auguste, 14–15
contemplation, 35, 43, 54, 84, 85, 87–91,
    110
conversion, 8, 24, 39, 84, 95
Cosmic Christ, 62, 66–73
courage, 110, 117–19, 136
creation, doctrine of, 57, 69, 72, 98, 107,
    109, 124, 125, 126
Cullmann, Oscar, 65

dance, 41
Dante Alighieri, 68
D'Arcy, Paula, 80

INDEX

"Dark Night," 91–93
Dawkins, Richard, 9
deduction, 12–13, 19
depression, 11, 92–93
deprivation, 110, 111, 113, 117
    creativity and, 118–19
Descartes, René, 14
devotions. *See* practice, spiritual
Dillard, Annie, 33, 109, 128
discipleship, 58, 73, 112, 117, 136
disciplines, spiritual, 43
Dostoyevsky, Fyodor, 15, 126

Eastern religious perspective, 26, 28–30, 96
Einstein, Albert, 121, 127
Eiseley, Loren, 16, 123
Eliade, Mircea, 44
Emerson, Ralph Waldo, 33
ESP, 40
eternal life, 132, 138
existentialism, 15
    theistic, 15
experience, religious, 37–46

faith, 10, 12, 16, 66, 110
fantasy literature, 20, 40
Feyerabend, Paul, 19
Foster, Richard, 43, 45, 86, 91, 126
Fox, Matthew, 33, 67
Francis of Assisi, 18, 32, 39, 55, 68, 115, 124
Frank, Jerome, 16
Freud, Sigmund, 10, 15, 16, 23
fundamentalism, Christian, 15, 16

Gallup Poll, 27
Garden of Eden, 124
generosity, 55–59
God
    and suffering, 106–10, 112
    as absent, 91–93
    as Divine Lover, 33, 34, 35, 112, 138
    as interventionist, 84–85
    as personal, 79–80
    attributes of, 7, 8
    belief in, 28
    character of, 65
    encounter with, 1
    enjoyment of, 3, 4
    existence of, 7, 12
    experience of, 1, 2, 4–5, 8, 22–35, 42, 48–55, 61–75, 77–93, 95–105, 106–19, 121–28
    images of, 25–26, 73–74, 78, 79
    intimacy with, 2, 8, 33, 124
    knowing, 1, 2
    knowledge of, 1, 13, 35
    presence of, 2, 3, 4, 5, 80, 90, 138
    proofs of, 7, 12
    titles of, 66, 74
Gödel, Kurt, 17, 19
Gordon, Arthur, 121, 122
Greeley, Andrew, 16, 26
group process, 45

Hanh, Thich Nhat, 53
Harnack, Adolf von, 70
Haught, John 125–26
healing, divine, 44
heaven, 132, 133, 137, 138
Hegel, G. W. F., 14
Heisenberg, Werner, 17, 19, 34
hell, 137–38
Hildegarde of Bingen, 67–68
Hitler, Adolf, 16, 32
Hobbes, Thomas, 30
holy, the, 39
Holy Spirit, 5, 24, 45, 46, 58, 73, 77, 96, 105, 114, 118, 130, 137
    gifts of, 2, 37–38, 44
Hügel, Friedrich von, 22–23, 78, 80–82, 116–17
Huvelin, Abbé, 10, 80
Huxley, Aldous, 17
hypnosis, 46

icons, 20
illness, 111
    Jesus and, 108
    mental, 46
    physical, 106–8
imagination, religious, 18, 19, 20, 39, 49, 68, 86–87, 96, 110

INDEX

incarnation, 69, 75, 81–82, 109
induction, 19
intuition, 19, 20, 68

James, William, 12, 17, 18, 24, 30, 39
Jesus Christ, 18, 29, 41, 57, 61–75, 81–82, 117, 123, 125, 129, 130, 134, 135, 136
    as Logos, 69, 70–73, 103
    as Suffering Servant, 107, 113
    as Wisdom, 69, 70, 71, 73
    the kingdom of God and, 129–33
Jesus Prayer, 88
joy, 35, 41, 136, 138
Julian of Norwich, 18, 68
Jung, Carl, 10, 11, 12, 16, 18, 20, 40, 114, 133

Kant, Immanuel, 13–14, 121
kataphatic tradition, 29, 33, 42, 43, 50, 82, 86
Keating, Thomas, 2, 88, 90, 104
Kelsey, Morton, 1, 2, 10, 17, 38–39, 131–32
Kidd, Sue Monk, 88–89
Kierkegaard, Søren, 15, 135
kingdom of God, 41, 58, 59, 63–64, 123, 129–38
Kübler-Ross, Elisabeth, 111
Kuhn, T. S., 17, 19

Lamott, Anne, 116
Lao Tzu, 74
Lectio Divina, 99–102, 103, 105
Lewis, C. S., 20, 46, 49
Loftus, John, 9
Lord's Prayer, 64, 89, 135, 136
love
    divine, 39, 41, 61, 66, 112, 136, 138
    human, 41, 58, 82–83
Loyola, Ignatius, 18, 29, 86
Luther, Martin, 18

materialism, reductionism, 10, 12, 14, 15, 16, 18, 19, 20, 24, 30, 34, 64
May, Gerald, 5
McLoughlin, William, 26. 27

meditation, 35, 43, 59, 84, 85, 85–87, 110
mediums, 46
Meister Eckhart, 33, 68
midlife crisis, 23, 24
monastic(ism), 45–46, 103
Moore, Thomas, 32
Muhammad, 40
mystical, mysticism, 16, 18, 26, 33, 39, 66–67, 78, 81, 125

nature, 121–28
neurosis, 46
Newton, Isaac, 19, 68
Nietzsche, Friedrich, 15–16
numinous, 39

old age, 111–12
oracles, 44
Otto, Rudolph, 39

Packer, James I., 1, 2
panentheism, 73–74
pantheism, 73
parapsychology, 16
Pascal, Blaise, 74
Paul (apostle), 8, 37–38, 39, 48, 53, 56, 58, 67, 69, 108, 109, 130, 135, 138
personality (psychological) types, 20, 133
Philo of Alexandria, 72
Plato, 13, 16, 18, 19, 29, 30, 40, 41, 71
play, playfulness, 123–24
positivism, 14–15
postmodernism, 12
practice, spiritual, 43, 78, 80, 82–84, 91
prayer, 8, 35, 59, 65–66, 77, 81, 82, 83, 84–85, 91, 110
    unanswered, 85
primal spirituality, 30–31
psychosis, 32, 46
psychotherapy, 5–6

Quakers, 43

reason, 12, 18, 71
reincarnation, 29, 40
religion, mature, 78, 79, 126
resurrection, 65, 66, 82, 109, 131, 137

INDEX

revivals and awakenings, 26–28
righteous(ness), 135
rituals, religious, 20, 31, 42–43, 63, 96–97
Rohr, Richard, 3, 4, 17, 67, 68, 114, 115
Rowling, J. K., 49

sacrament(al), 42, 48, 55, 59, 95, 96, 99, 110, 114, 125, 126
    Bible as, 99
    nature as, 126
sacred, the, 39, 48, 123
sacrifice, 123
Sanford, John, 64
Sartre, Jean-Paul, 10
scripture. *See* Bible
second half of life, 3–4
Sermon on the Mount, 52, 57, 131–33
shaman, 44
sickness, 16, 106, 108
skepticism, 9, 12, 13, 14
Slater, Philip, 56
soul, 13, 114
spiritual gifts. *See* charismatic gifts
spiritual journey, 4–5, 8–9, 115
spirituality, 4–6, 17, 18, 37
Spong, John Shelby, 80
stewardship, 57–59
Stoics, 71
suffering, 35, 40, 106–19
    and sin, 106–8
    creative, 110–14
    redemptive, 113–14
    vicarious, 107, 113

telepathy, 40
Temple, William, 96
ten Boom, Corrie, 113
Tertullian, 124

thin places, 48–49
Thoreau, Henry David, 33
Tolkien, J. R. R., 20
Torah, 70, 83
Tournier, Paul, 110, 112, 117, 118
Traherne, Thomas, 33
Transcendental Meditation, 26
transformation, spiritual, 34, 35, 41–42, 49, 52, 56, 59, 66, 80, 82, 83, 90, 97, 105, 112
Trinity, the, 62
Two Books, 124

unconscious, the, 40, 89, 90, 104
Underhill, Evelyn, 81–82

Virgin Birth, 82
visions, 8, 39, 44, 64
von Hügel, Friedrich. *See* Hügel, Friedrich von

Walls, Andrew, 75
Walsh, Roger, 16
Watts, Alan, 123–24
Western religious perspective, 29, 32–35, 96
Westminster Shorter Catechism, 3
Whitman, Walt, 33
Whyte, L. L., 14
Wickes, Francis, 20
Wilber, Ken, 3
Williams, Charles, 135
wonder, 41, 121–23
Wordsworth, William, 33
worship, corporate, 77, 78, 83, 95–97

yoga, 26, 87

www.ingramcontent.com/pod-product-compliance
Lightning Source LLC
Chambersburg PA
CBHW070910160426
43193CB00011B/1417